Malcolm Shuttleworth

Classroom Games

Spielend Englisch lernen

Anaconda

Die Deutsche Nationalbibliothek verzeichnet diese Publikation
in der Deutschen Nationalbibliografie; detaillierte bibliografische Daten
sind im Internet unter http://dnb.d-nb.de abrufbar.

© 2014 Anaconda Verlag GmbH, Köln
Alle Rechte vorbehalten.
Umschlagmotiv: iStockphoto.com
Umschlaggestaltung: dyadesign, Düsseldorf, www.dya.de
Satz und Layout: Andreas Paqué, Ebergötzen, www.paque.de
Printed in Czech Republic 2014
ISBN 978-3-7306-0094-8
www.anacondaverlag.de
info@anacondaverlag.de

Vorwort

Classroom Games ist eine Sammlung von Spielen, die ich in den über 10 Jahren meiner Arbeit als Sprachlehrer (hauptsächlich in der Erwachsenenbildung) zusammengetragen, selbst erfunden, adaptiert und bearbeitet habe.

Spiele im Klassenzimmer – egal ob in der Schule, im Abendkurs oder in der Nachhilfestunde – lockern die Stimmung, fördern die Gruppendynamik oder dienen der Entspannung nach besonders schwierigen Unterrichtsstunden. Man kann sie je nach Spiel alleine, zu zweit oder in größeren Gruppen spielen oder spielen lassen. Sie schulen Vokabeln und Grammatik außerhalb des Lehrbuchs beim Hören, Sprechen und Schreiben. Und natürlich kann man sie auch außerhalb des Unterrichts verwenden, zum Spielen in der Familie oder für den Spieleabend mit Freunden!

Die meisten meiner „classroom games" können als einfache Kopiervorlagen genutzt und in der Klasse verteilt werden. Für einige, zum Beispiel das „50/50 game", braucht man eine Tafel.

Detaillierte Spielanleitungen stehen vor jedem der 30 Spiele, von denen manche gleich als Set von zwei, drei oder mehr Spielen derselben Art daherkommen (im Inhaltsverzeichnis habe ich die jeweilige Anzahl in Klammern hinter das Spiel geschrieben).

Am Ende des Buches finden sich für einige Spiele außerdem offene Spielvorlagen („templates"), die je nach Gruppe, Alter der Schüler oder Wissensstand mit eigenem Material gefüllt und den Bedürfnissen angepasst werden können.

Und nun wünsche ich viel Spaß beim Ausprobieren, Rätseln und Entdecken!

Odenthal im Juni 2014

Malcolm Shuttleworth

Contents

Game No. 1
50/50 game

Oh, the agony of choice!

WELCOME TO HELL
⬅ ETERNAL DAMNATION
ROT IN HELL ➡
⬇ FLAMETHROWER AGONY

How to play the game

Preparation: Pick two teams, teams A and B.

The idea of the game: Each team is given a word or expression and two alternative definitions. If a team guesses the correct definition they get a point. The team with the most points wins the game.

Playing the game: Say the word or expression and write down the two definitions on the board. Give the teams a little time to discuss and decide on their answers.

(N. B. The underlined words are the correct answers.)

Team A

1. **erstwhile**
   first/<u>former</u>

2. **tryst**
   <u>meeting</u>/bad

3. **bog-standard**
   exclusive/<u>normal</u>

4. **codswallop**
   excellent!/<u>rubbish!</u>

5. **gaffer**
   tape/<u>boss</u>

6. **naff**
   <u>useless</u>/brilliant

7. **a plonker**
   a tool/<u>an idiot</u>

8. **slowcoach**
   a slow vehicle/<u>a slow person</u>

9. **yonks**
   Americans/<u>a long time</u>

10. **pernickety**
    dirty/<u>fussy</u>

Team B

1. **kerfuffle**
   <u>fuss</u>/party

2. **chuffed**
   annoyed/<u>pleased</u>

3. **brass monkey weather**
   <u>cold</u>/hot

4. **French letter**
   a cocktail/<u>a condom</u>

5. **a johnny**
   <u>a condom</u>/a tool

6. **nowt**
   many/<u>none</u>

7. **a scrubber**
   <u>a common woman</u>/a tool

8. **sweet FA**
   <u>nothing</u>/everything

9. **a strop**
   a leather belt/<u>rage</u>

10. **a niff**
    <u>a smell</u>/a strong drink

Team A

1. **in a jiffy**
   <u>in a moment</u>/never

2. **clout**
   <u>influence</u>/noise

3. **a barb**
   food/<u>insult</u>

4. **plucky**
   cowardly/<u>brave</u>

5. **(to) peg out**
   (to) follow/<u>(to) die</u>

6. **flush**
   rich/<u>poor</u>

7. **double Dutch**
   <u>incomprehensible</u>/clear

8. **(to) tamper**
   (to) slow down/<u>(to) interfere</u>

9. **seedy**
   full of seeds/<u>dirty & cheap</u>

10. **(to) totter**
    (to) drink heavily/
    <u>(to) walk unsteadily</u>

Team B

1. **a crooner**
   <u>an old singer</u>/a tall glass

2. **tickled pink**
   <u>pleased</u>/not amused

3. **spitting blood**
   <u>incredibly angry</u>/horny

4. **(to) flap**
   <u>(to) panic</u>/(to) wave

5. **a wench**
   <u>young girl</u>/a tool

6. **crestfallen**
   <u>beautiful</u>/disappointed

7. **a tall story**
   long/<u>lies</u>

8. **a tiff**
   <u>an argument</u>/a joint

9. **jammy**
   <u>really lucky</u>/sticky

10. **glum**
    <u>really sad</u>/asleep

Team A

1. **dog rough**
   <u>really ugly</u>/really strong

2. **(to) take umbrage**
   <u>(to) be offended</u>/(to) steal

3. **a dipstick**
   <u>an idiot</u>/a foodstuff

4. **loaded**
   ill/<u>rich</u>

5. **lolly**
   alcohol/<u>money</u>

6. **a bollocking**
   <u>a telling off</u>/sex

7. **a bird**
   a friend/<u>a girlfriend</u>

8. **don't give a toss**
   don't take part/<u>don't care</u>

9. **bladdered**
   ready for a pee/<u>really drunk</u>

10. **skint**
    very thin/<u>having no money</u>

Team B

1. **barking**
   <u>mad</u>/noisy

2. **hapless**
   <u>unfortunate</u>/uncaring

3. **squiffy**
   soft/<u>rather drunk</u>

4. **'What's the damage?'**
   <u>how much?</u>/what's that?

5. **a newt**
   a youth/<u>a small lizard</u>

6. **a dressing down**
   nightshirt/<u>a telling off</u>

7. **a cradle snatcher**
   a thief/<u>someone who dates someone much younger than themselves</u>

8. **a barney**
   <u>an argument</u>/a sandwich

9. **(to) hump**
   <u>(to) have sex</u>/(to) complain

10. **lovely jubbly!**
    <u>wonderful!</u>/good night!

Team A

1. **puny**
   <u>weak</u>/stupid

2. **dicey**
   <u>dangerous</u>/noisy

3. **lippy**
   kissable/<u>cheeky</u>

4. **a quid**
   a fish/<u>a pound</u>

5. **crotchety**
   slowly/<u>ill-tempered</u>

6. **an errand**
   <u>a job</u>/a type of food

7. **going Dutch**
   <u>paying 50/50</u>/going crazy

8. **(to) ransack**
   (to) go quicker/<u>(to) plunder</u>

9. **a windfall**
   debris/<u>an unexpected gain</u>

10. **a good hiding**
    a secret place/<u>a battering</u>

Team B

1. **daft**
   <u>stupid</u>/cold

2. **bonkers**
   <u>crazy</u>/sausages

3. **a basket case**
   a shopping bag/<u>crazy</u>

4. **a stiff**
   a strong drink/<u>a corpse</u>

5. **snuffed it**
   <u>dead</u>/refused it

6. **a Hooray Henry**
   <u>a rich snob</u>/a hero

7. **(to) fudge**
   (to) extend/<u>(to) cheat</u>

8. **game**
   <u>willing</u>/tired

9. **'You get on my wick!'**
   <u>you annoy me!</u>/you're hot!

10. **a fence**
    an old friend/<u>a crook</u>

Team A

1. **soppy**
   hopelessly romantic/arrogant

2. **a sticky patch**
   a leak/a bad period

3. **(to) make a meal of something**
   (to) make the best of/
   (to) over-exaggerate

4. **(to) meet your match**
   (to) meet your future partner/
   (to) come up against someone
   better than you

5. **fat chance!**
   a good chance/no chance

6. **a job lot**
   lots of different things/
   a temporary job

7. **(to) pop the question**
   (to) refuse to answer/
   (to) propose marriage

8. **off by heart**
   from memory/forgotten

9. **nothing doing**
   I'm bored/I won't do it!

10. **(to have) a short fuse**
    (to) be small/
    (to) be easily annoyed

Team B

1. **cranky**
   lazy/irritable

2. **a dive**
   a horrible place/a lie

3. **a hole**
   a dirty place/a hiding place

4. **(to) bump off**
   (to) forget/(to) kill

5. **yellow-bellied**
   cowardly/sick

6. **brekkers**
   workmen/breakfast

7. **square**
   conservative/tired

8. **(to) smell a rat**
   (to) dislike someone/(to) suspect
   that something is not right

9. **(to) nod off**
   (to) fall asleep/(to) say 'yes'

10. **(to) nobble**
    (to) eat/(to) interfere with

Team A

1. **tosh**
   great/<u>rubbish</u>

2. **a drip**
   <u>an idiot</u>/a tool

3. **no frills**
   expensive/<u>cheap</u>

4. **jerry built**
   stable/<u>instable</u>

5. **a prat**
   a biscuit/<u>an idiot</u>

6. **a good egg**
   <u>a good person</u>/a good club

7. **(to) dawdle**
   (to) look at/<u>(to) go slow</u>

8. **(to) have kittens**
   (to) laugh/<u>(to) panic</u>

9. **button it**
   move faster/<u>shut up</u>

10. **crumpet**
    a small bed/<u>women</u>

Team B

1. **graft**
   <u>work</u>/party

2. **carping**
   snoring/<u>moaning</u>

3. **rank**
   brilliant/<u>awful</u>

4. **the drink**
   bed/<u>water</u>

5. **a good craic**
   <u>a good time</u>/a good person

6. **past it**
   too late/<u>too old</u>

7. **(to) gawp**
   <u>(to) look at</u>/(to) laugh

8. **a bard**
   a <u>poet</u>/a big meal

9. **40 winks**
   a quick meal/<u>a short sleep</u>

10. **snakebite**
    <u>alcohol</u>/sex

Team A

1. **that takes the biscuit!**
   that's unbelievable!/
   that's nonsense!

2. **a bap**
   a tool/a bread roll

3. **'Use your loaf!'**
   think!/work!

4. **'Speak up!'**
   speak louder/tell the truth

5. **a whinger**
   a handle/a complainer

6. **a knobhead**
   part of an engine/an idiot

7. **(to) slouch**
   (to) lie around/(to) go quickly

8. **(to) fall head over heels**
   (to) steal/(to) fall in love

9. **(to) spark someone's lights out**
   (to) tell a secret/
   (to) hit someone

10. **bollocks!**
    rubbish!/bravo!

Team B

1. **two-timing**
   cheating on your boyfriend/
   girlfriend/doing two jobs

2. **costly**
   cheap/expensive

3. **twaddle**
   old rags/nonsense

4. **(to) pass away**
   (to) die/(to) leave

5. **a lecher**
   a dirty old man/a tool

6. **'You are a brick!'**
   you are great!/you are an idiot!

7. **(to) doctor**
   (to) fake/(to) sympathise

8. **I. O. U.**
   I love you/I owe you money

9. **dishy**
   very handsome/very clean

10. **stuffy**
    airless/big

Team A

1. **on the dot**
   upside down/<u>punctual</u>

2. **(to) hog**
   <u>(to) keep for oneself</u>/(to) cry

3. **offspring**
   <u>children</u>/parents

4. **fisticuffs**
   <u>a fight</u>/a party

5. **crazy paving**
   a children's game/
   <u>stone paving for gardens</u>

6. **(to) pin back your lugholes**
   <u>(to) listen</u>/(to) wash your hair

7. **a wino**
   <u>a drunk</u>/a special kind of wine

8. **tight-fisted**
   angry/<u>penny-pinching</u>

9. **a rozzer**
   a tramp/<u>a policeman</u>

10. **(to) bar**
    <u>(to) refuse entry</u>/(to) welcome

Team B

1. **in a rut**
   <u>depressed</u>/drunk

2. **inundated**
   <u>overwhelmed</u>/happy

3. **foolproof**
   <u>100% safe</u>/unsafe

4. **(to) fly off the handle**
   (to) move quickly/
   <u>(to) lose one's temper</u>

5. **bottle**
   <u>nerve</u>/jealousy

6. **(to) rummage**
   <u>(to) search quickly through</u>/
   (to) shout

7. **stingy**
   <u>penny-pinching</u>/sentimental

8. **(to be) in hock**
   <u>(to) owe money</u>/(to) be in love

9. **choked**
   <u>very emotional</u>/full

10. **(to) welsh on a deal**
    <u>(to) go back on a deal</u>/
    (to) conclude a deal

Team A

1. **flush**
   having lots of money/poor

2. **a fag**
   a bath/a cigarette

3. **gruff**
   bad-tempered/happy

4. **in the blink of an eye**
   slowly/quickly

5. **an Indian summer**
   a good summer/a late summer

6. **route one**
   direct/indirect

7. **touch and go**
   unsure/sure

8. **take someone down
   a peg or two**
   teach someone a lesson/
   help someone

9. **'Good riddance!'**
   glad to see the back of you!/
   good luck!

10. **(to) ditch someone**
    (to) help someone/
    (to) end a relationship

Team B

1. **living from hand to mouth**
   living from one day to the next/
   living like a king

2. **(to) wheeze**
   (to) breath heavily/
   (to) trick someone

3. **muffled**
   clear/unclear

4. **lacklustre**
   passionately/without passion

5. **a doubting Thomas**
   a disbeliever/a bad person

6. **(to) fiddle**
   (to) cheat/
   (to) give someone a present

7. **a windbag**
   a piece of technical equipment/
   someone who talks a lot

8. **broody**
   longing for a child/unhelpful

9. **'Look lively!'**
   let's dance!/let's get moving!

10. **slender**
    slim/fat

Team A

1. **tatty**
   <u>old and worn</u>/stylish

2. **broke**
   <u>poor</u>/rich

3. **'Pardon my French'**
   sorry for the bad food/
   <u>excuse my swearing</u>

4. **'Get off my back!'**
   stop making fun of me!/
   <u>stop criticising me!</u>

5. **(to) give someone grief**
   (to) sympathise/
   <u>(to) complain non-stop</u>

6. **a sub**
   <u>money in advance</u>/a fine

7. **cloak and dagger**
   <u>secretly</u>/openly

8. **taking the Michael**
   impersonating someone/
   <u>making fun of someone</u>

9. **a spin doctor**
   <u>a political advisor</u>/a bad doctor

10. **(to) hoodwink**
    <u>(to) deceive</u>/(to) amuse

Team B

1. **natty**
   <u>well-dressed</u>/badly dressed

2. **a raving loony**
   <u>a madman</u>/a funny person

3. **blackballed**
   <u>refused membership</u>
   <u>(i. e. to club)</u>/hated

4. **dire**
   expensive/<u>terrible</u>

5. **cutthroat**
   quick/<u>highly competitive</u>

6. **poxy**
   <u>awful</u>/wonderful

7. **a wind-up**
   <u>a hoax</u>/a piece of equipment

8. **(to) hang fire**
   <u>(to) stop firing</u>/
   (to) commence firing

9. **kinky**
   crazy/<u>sexually perverted</u>

10. **(to) maroon**
    <u>(to) strand (on a desert island)</u>/
    (to) mimic

Game No. 2
Bizarre world records

'She's entered the nagging World Championships!'

How to play the game

Teams/individuals.

Preparation: Photocopy the game.

The idea of the game: To get points by guessing the bizarre world records.

Playing the game: Give the teams/individuals time to complete the sheet. If a team/individual has the correct answer, they get three points. If no one has the correct answer, the team/individual who is closest gets one point. The team/individual with the most points wins the game.

1. Typing to one million

two thousand four hundred and fifty
two thousand four hundred and fifty-one
two thousand four hundred and fifty-two
two thousand four hundred and fifty-three
two thousand four hundred and fifty-four
two thousand four hundred and fifty-five
two thousand four hundred and fifty-six
two thousand four hundred and fifty-seven
two thousand four hundred and fifty-eight
two thousand four hundred and fifty-nine

How long:

_____

2. World's largest house of cards

How many cards:

_____

3. Most t-shirts worn at one time

How many:

_____

4. World's largest rubber band ball

How many rubber bands: _____

5. World's oldest prostitute

How old:

_____

6. World's oldest father

How old:

_____

7. World's largest naked photo shoot

How many people: _____

8. World's highest bungee jump

How many metres:

_____

1. Fastest time to duct tape a person to the wall

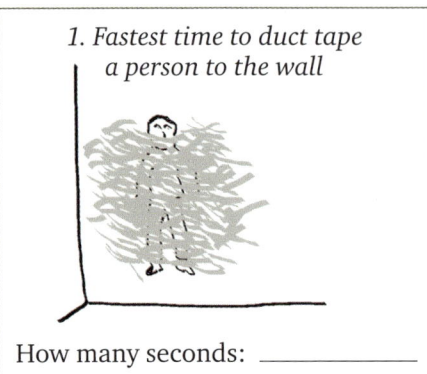

How many seconds: _____

2. Most t-shirts folded in one minute

How many: _____

3. World's longest handshake

How long: _____

4. Most spoons balanced on the face

How many: _____

5. Biggest English breakfast eaten

How many kilos: _____

6. Most people in a Smart car

How many: _____

7. Fastest time to dress a Barbie doll

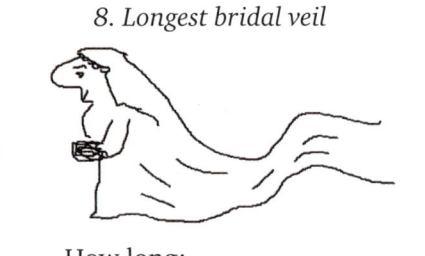

How many seconds: _____

8. Longest bridal veil

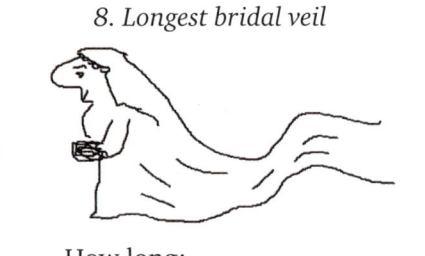

How long: _____

1. Sitting in a bath of ice

How many minutes: _____

2. Lifting weights with an ear

How many kilos:

_____

3. Most straws in the mouth

How many: _____

4. Most cosmetic surgery operations

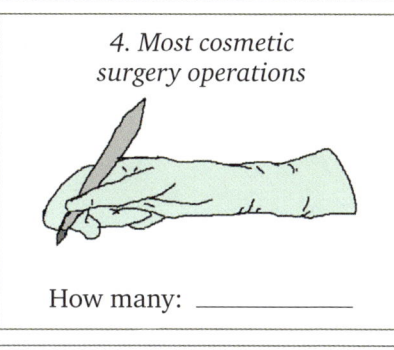

How many: _____

5. Most times married

How many times: _____

6. Simultaneous kissing

How many people: _____

7. Most people dressed as Santa Claus

How many people:

_____

8. Most litres of beer glasses carried by a woman

How many:

_____

1. World's biggest barbecue

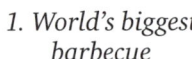

How many people brought food and cooked:

_____

2. World's longest bridge

How long: _____ km

3. World record number of body piercings

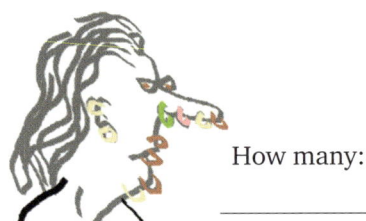

How many:

_____

4. Juggling

Most balls kept in the air at one time:

_____

5. Heaviest car balanced on the head

How many kilos:

_____

6. Highest stiletto

How many cm: _____

7. World's oldest person

How old:

_____

8. World's biggest cupcake

How many kilos:

_____

1. Running 100 metres on ice

How many seconds: _____

2. Fastest time to eat a 12" pizza

How many seconds: _____

3. Most cockroaches eaten in one minute

How many: _____

4. Heaviest aircraft pulled by one man

How many tons: _____

5. Most press-ups using the back of the hands in one hour

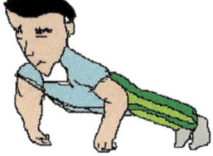

How many: _____

6. World's longest cigar

How long: _____

7. World's biggest omelette

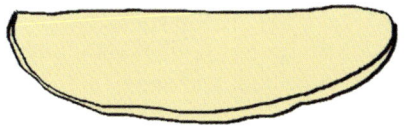

How many: _____

8. World's biggest onion

How many kilos:

_____

Game No. 3
Numbers quiz

'What do you mean this is my lucky number?'

How to play the game

Teams/individuals.

Preparation: Photocopy the game.

The idea of the game: The idea of the game is NOT to get points.

Playing the game: Each team/individual fills in the quiz sheet. The idea is to get as close as possible to the correct answer. A correct answer means no points. Otherwise, if, for example, the answer is 10 and a team/individual guesses 6, they score four points, etc.

The team/individual with **the least number** of points wins the game.

Team Name: _____

Questions	Answers	Points
1. How many days in April, May and June?		
2. How many different values of British coins are in circulation?		
3. Which A do you get if you halve a sheet of A4 paper?		
4. What's 20% of 2000?		
5. How many bits in a byte?		
6. How many symphonies did Beethoven write?		
7. How many legs on an ant?		
8. How many sides on a 50 pence piece?		
9. How many stripes on the Stars & Stripes?		
10. Queen Victoria reigned for how many years?		
11. What is the gestation period in days of the African elephant?		
12. How many mm in a km?		
13. How many capsules on the London Eye?		
14. In what year was Walt Disney's Jungle Book film released?		
15. How many players on the court in a basketball team?		
	Team Score:	

Team Name: _____

Questions	Answers	Points
1. How many lives does a cat have?		
2. How many dominoes in a normal set?		
3. How many wheels on a unicycle?		
4. What's the maximum number of golf clubs you can use in a tournament?		
5. If you are happy you are on cloud what?		
6. How many inches in a yard?		
7. How many seasons in Vivaldi's composition?		
8. How many tails on a Manx cat?		
9. How many eyes on a cyclops?		
10. To the nearest kilometre, how long is the Channel Tunnel?		
11. How old was the oldest man in space?		
12. How many spikes on the Statue of Liberty's head?		
13. How many wheels on a tandem?		
14. How many plays did Shakespeare write?		
15. Around the world in how many days?		
	Team Score:	

Team Name: _____

Questions	Answers	Points
1. What does the Roman number L stand for?		
2. How many questions must you answer correctly to win one million on 'Who Wants To Be A Millionaire'?		
3. What's the maximum number you can score with three darts?		
4. Unlucky …		
5. How many Nobel prizes are presented each year?		
6. If you are blissfully happy, you are in _____ heaven.		
7. How many seconds in an hour?		
8. How many hours in a week?		
9. How many black keys on a standard piano?		
10. How many colours in a rainbow?		
11. How many reindeer does Santa's sleigh have?		
12. How many strings on a 12-string guitar?		
13. The lowest temperature ever recorded on Earth was minus what?		
14. What is the highest temperature recorded on Earth?		
15. What is Russia's population to the nearest million?		
	Team Score:	

Game No. 4
Odd man out

'He always has to be different!'

How to play the game

Teams/individuals.

The idea of the game: To get points by identifying the odd man out.

Playing the game: Write down the four words on the board. The first team/individual to guess the odd man out AND give the reason why gets a point. The team/individual with most points wins the game.

1.	Otto	Mum	Tom	Dad
2.	Man	Assessment	City	Call
3.	Match	Game	Play	Set
4.	Die	Fall	Boot	New
5.	Talk	Speak	Tell	Write
6.	Happy	Grumpy	Moody	Sleepy
7.	King	Queen	Prince	Supertramp
8.	2010	1804	2400	2000
9.	George Michael	Rod Stewart	Cliff Richard	Tom Jones
10.	Nürnberg	Berlin	Frankfurt	Thüringen
11.	Knife	Junction	Time	Bone
12.	Street	James	Personal	Call
13.	Golf	Handball	Football	Basketball
14.	York	Delhi	Hampshire	Boston
15.	Chester	Made	Kind	Woman

1.	River	Arms	Cot	Pram
2.	Carol	Anita	Anna	Bob
3.	Ronald Reagan	John F. Kennedy	Martin Luther King	Yitzhak Rabin
4.	Snow	Ice Cubes	Ice Cream	Cocoa
5	Umbrellas	Rain	Petrol Prices	Taxes
6.	Brazil	Argentina	America	Australia
7.	Andrew	Edward	Anne	George
8.	Abba	The Corrs	Queen	Blondie
9.	Sweden	Denmark	UK	Germany
10.	Die Toten Hosen	Gildo Horn	Lena	Stefan Raab
11.	Spider	Ant	Beetle	Bee
12.	Heaven 17	Boyz 11 Men	4 Non Blondes	Men At Work
13.	Bahamas	Jamaica	Indonesia	Thailand
14.	Roy	Charlie	Lesley	Stevie
15.	Italy	Spanish	France	Germany

Game No. 5
True or false?

Q. Canberra is the
   capital of Australia.

a. true
b. false
c. who cares?

'Ok, who's the comedian?'

How to play the game

Preparation: Pick two or more teams. Each team starts with 20 points. Write the team names and the points on the board.

The idea of the game: To answer true or false questions and to gamble points successfully.

Playing the game: Ask each team a true or false question in turn. The number of rounds depends on the time available. Teams can gamble up to five points on their answers. If they answer correctly, the points are added to their score. If they answer incorrectly, the points are subtracted. Any team that reaches zero points is out of the game.

All or nothing question: The final question is for all teams and they can now bet up to as many points as they have on the board. Teams must write down their answers and decide how many points they want to gamble.

Do they play safe if they are in the lead? Do they go for broke? The team with the most points after the all or nothing question wins the game.

29

1. Camels are born without humps.

2. Mel Gibson was one of 10 children.

3. Sharks are immune to all known diseases.

4. 1000 quarter-pound hamburgers can be made out of one cow.

5. 'Dr Jekyll and Mr Hyde' is the most filmed story of all time.

6. Cats are the most popular pet in America.

7. Only male mosquitoes bite.

8. The only thing that can destroy a diamond is intense heat.

9. An octopus has two hearts.

10. Beethoven had a photographic memory.

11. Krakow has a Pope John Paul II airport.

12. Boxer George Foreman named all his four sons George.

13. Lettuce is 85% water.

14. Beef is the most popular kind of meat in the world.

15. Walt Disney was afraid of mice.

All or nothing last question:

The loudest animal in the world is the African elephant.

1. The first Englishman to be killed in a plane crash was Charles Rolls of Rolls-Royce fame.

2. Blues legend Muddy Waters was the first recording artist to receive a gold disc.

3. The first supermarket in the world was in America.

4. The world's first cash machine was in London, England.

5. A hippo is born under water.

6. Vincent Van Gogh only sold one painting while he was alive.

7. No word in the English language rhymes with pint.

8. The hummingbird is the only bird that can fly backwards.

9. There was once a town in West Virginia called '9'.

10. The average person spends two months of their lifetime waiting for traffic lights to change.

11. The most visited country in the world is the USA.

12. There is a George Bush airport in Houston.

13. 13 people have walked on the moon.

14. Winston Churchill had a stammer when he was a young boy.

15. Bill Clinton & Bill Gates have photographic memories.

All or nothing last question:

The last song Elvis sang in public was 'My Way'.

1. Our nose, eyes and ears never stop growing until the day we die.

2. The most common first name in the world is Mohammed.

3. No word in the English language has five consecutive letters that are vowels.

4. If a month starts on a Sunday it will contain Friday the 13th.

5. There are only 25 countries worldwide in which people drive on the left-hand side of the road.

6. The youngest ever Pope was only 12 years old.

7. Diamond is the hardest natural substance on earth.

8. More than 1.5 million people die each year from malaria.

9. More than a third of adults hit the snooze button at least three times before they get up.

10. In the English version of the game 'Monopoly', Old Kent Road is the most valuable property.

11. Bagpipes were invented not by the Scottish, but by the Romans.

12. 'Happy Birthday' was the first song to be performed in outer space, sung by the Apollo IX astronauts on March 8, 1969.

13. Jimi Hendrix, Janis Joplin, and Jim Morrison were all 26 years old when they died.

14. The 1st feature-length animated film released by Disney Studios was 'The Jungle Book'.

15. Jim Morrison (of the 60's rock group The Doors) was the first rock star to be arrested on stage.

All or nothing last question:

China's Beijing Duck Restaurant can seat 8,000 people at one time.

1. Australia is the only country that is also a continent.

2. According to German researchers, the risk of heart attack is higher on a Sunday than any other day of the week.

3. It takes 17 muscles to frown – 43 to smile.

4. A zebra is black with white stripes.

5. German Shepherds bite humans more than any other breed of dog.

6. Large kangaroos cover more than 10 metres with each jump.

7. No word in the English language rhymes with orange.

8. 'Rhythms' is the longest English word without a vowel.

9. The shortest war on record, between Britain and Zanzibar in 1896, lasted just 38 hours.

10. There are over 200 rooms in the White House.

11. Cashews are the only nuts mentioned in the Bible.

12. When Coca Cola was first produced it was green.

13. The lead singer of the band Toto shot and killed himself in a game of Russian Roulette in 1978. His last words were, 'Don't worry, it's not loaded.'

14. The parachute was invented by Leonardo da Vinci.

15. Disney World is bigger than the world's 15 smallest countries.

All or nothing last question:

Two out of every ten people who come to a party in your home will look in your bathroom cabinet.

1. There was once a Society for the Prevention of People Being Buried Alive.

2. You share your birthday with at least 90 million others.

3. Only seven men have ever known the formula for Coca-Cola. Today only two men are in on the secret, and they take the precaution of never travelling in the same aircraft.

4. The Greek national anthem has 148 verses.

5. Beethoven was once arrested for being a tramp.

6. When the Star Wars director George Lucas said the legendary words 'May the force be with you' at a press conference, an interpreter for the German TV channel N24 translated the words as 'Am 4. Mai sind wir bei Ihnen.'

7. According to an old law, women in Memphis, Tennessee were only allowed to drive if a man walked in front of the car waving a red flag as a warning sign to other drivers.

8. An average woman spends 16 days of her life rummaging in her handbag.

9. Franz Beckenbauer has already appeared in advertisements for five different makes of car.

10. Half of the dog owners in Germany buy Christmas presents for their dogs.

11. In Newfoundland, Canada there is a place called 'Vibrator'.

12. In the German telephone directories there are around 1.2 million different surnames.

13. Prince William's nickname when he was at St Andrews University was 'Big Willy'.

14. A 1997 survey found that about 90% of American workers would like to fire their boss.

15. 47% of all statistics are made up.

All or nothing last question:

Elvis Presley never toured outside the United States.

Double trouble quiz

'I am not drunk! Why don't you both believe me?'

How to play the game

Teams/individuals.

Preparation: Photocopy the game and distribute it among the teams/individuals.

The idea of the game: To get points by answering the questions correctly.

Playing the game: Give the teams/individuals a few minutes to complete the quiz. Award three points for every correct answer. If no one has the correct answer, award one point to the team/individual that is closest. The team/individual with the most points wins the game.

1. ___ % of all newly-opened restaurants fail in the first year. Of the ones that survive, ___ % fail in the second year.

2. King Mongut of Siam had _____ wives, but was quoted as saying he only loved ____ of them.

3. In the 1950s ___ % of chickens in Europe were free-range. By 1980 it was only ___ %.

4. ___ million blood cells are produced and destroyed in the human body every _____.

5. Every year _____ people choke to death on _____.

6. In Kentucky ___ % of people getting married for the first time are under _____ years of age.

7. Americans eat approximately ____ billion _____ every year.

8. _____ is the most common name in ___ _____.

9. _____ bees are all _____.

10. ___% of the workers building the Panama Canal – which opened in 1914 – suffered from _____.

11. In Africa more people are killed by _____ than by _____.

12. Julio Iglesias once had five gallons of water flown from Miami to _____ so he could wash his _____.

13. _____ are the biggest-selling frozen vegetable in ___ _____.

14. ___ _____ is 300,300 times bigger than ____ _____.

15. There are _____ thousand living organisms in a glass of _____.

16. The average _____ sleeps _____ a day.

17. A typical American eats ___ pigs in _____.

18. 4,000 years ago in _____, the penalty for killing a cat was _____.

19. When left alone with a tea cosy, _____ % of _____ will put it on their heads.

20. During the _____ World War, the American automobile industry produced _____ cars.

Game No. 7
Words quiz

I know this one....

How to play the game

Teams/individuals.

Preparation: Photocopy the game and distribute it among the teams/individuals.

The idea of the game: To get points by knowing words.

Playing the game: Give the teams/individuals a few minutes to complete the quiz. Award one point for every word a team/individual knows. Award three points to any team/individual that is the only one who knows a word. The team/individual with the most points wins the game.

The most beautiful English words

(Chosen by more than 7,000 students in 46 countries.)

1. mother		11. hope	
2. passion		12. rainbow	
3. smile		13. tickle	
4. eternity		14. paradox	
5. destiny		15. sophisticated	
6. lullaby		16. cute	
7. liberty		17. cosy	
8. peace		18. hilarious	
9. tranquillity		19. lollipop	
10. sweetheart		20. bumblebee	

21. flabbergasted	
22. hiccup	
23. hen night	
24. hippopotamus	
25. whoops	
26. butterfly	
27. peek-a-boo	
28. shipshape	
29. gorgeous	
30. bubble	

Young and old vocabulary

1. pension	
2. milk teeth	
3. healthy	
4. grandparents	
5. grandchildren	
6. zimmer frame	
7. dummy	
8. pocket money	
9. false teeth	
10. bib	

11. slide	
12. old-age pension	
13. care home	
14. playground	
15. exams	
16. meals on wheels	
17. social worker	
18. midwife	
19. swing	
20. old folks' home	

21. retirement	
22. potty training	
23. spot	
24. first kiss	
25. school report	
26. wedding anniversary	
27. retirement home	
28. spry	
29. sweets	
30. cry-baby	

Pub vocabulary

1. a pub crawl	
2. 'It's your round!'	
3. drayman	
4. 'Last orders!'	
5. draught beer	
6. bottled beer	
7. pork scratchings	
8. crisps	
9. pool	
10. darts	

11. spirits	
12. beer mat	
13. landlord	
14. ashtray	
15. barmaid	
16. a pint	
17. a dive	
18. barrels	
19. cellar	
20. country pub	

21. brewery	
22. hand pump	
23. hops	
24. pay at the bar	
25. pub grub	
26. hangover	
27. bartender	
28. underage drinking	
29. happy hour	
30. binge drinking	

Shopping vocabulary

1. shopping trolley		11. out of stock	
2. the till		12. down payment	
3. receipt		13. instalments	
4. shoplifter		14. interest free credit	
5. poultry		15. special offer	
6. scales		16. sale	
7. check out		17. closing down sale	
8. shop assistant		18. clearance sale	
9. store detective		19. barcode	
10. in stock		20. newsagent	

21. off licence	
22. discount	
23. VAT	
24. deposit	
25. shelves	
26. aisles	
27. shopping basket	
28. small change	
29. short-changed	
30. reduced	

Holiday vocabulary

1. currency	
2. long-haul flight	
3. domestic flight	
4. a leg of a journey	
5. (to be) frisked	
6. B&B	
7. half board	
8. full board	
9. self catering	
10. abroad	

11. turbulence	
12. suntan	
13. phrasebook	
14. off the beaten track	
15. (to) get ripped off	
16. package holiday	
17. off-peak	
18. flight	
19. duty free	
20. customs	

21. local cuisine	
22. local knowledge	
23. guided tour	
24. pickpocket	
25. tourist attraction	
26. chambermaid	
27. pool bar	
28. the old town	
29. holiday romance	
30. tour operator	

One minute all-out

Ready, steady, go!

How to play the game

Teams.

Preparation: Toss a coin to see which team starts, decide how many rounds there will be.

The idea of the game: To get points by naming as many words as possible beginning with a certain letter.

Playing the game: A team chooses two numbers from 1 to 26. One for the letter and one for the category. They then have one minute (use a stopwatch) to name as many words in that category beginning with the letter they have been given. The team with the most points wins the game.

	Letter	Category
1.	B	Female singers
2.	C	Male singers
3.	D	Musicals
4.	F	Films
5.	P	Places in Germany
6.	S	Places in Great Britain
7.	S	Football teams
8.	P	Sports
9.	G	Drinks
10.	R	Food
11.	A	Boys' names
12.	E	Girls' names
13.	D	Jobs
14.	L	Animals
15.	T	Travel
16.	F	Things that are round
17.	S	Things that are square
18.	C	Musical things
19.	B	Black things
20.	D	Red things
21.	N	Things in a kitchen
22.	B	Electrical things
23.	A	Things that are loud
24.	M	Toys
25.	F	Cartoon characters
26.	B	Female singers

Game No. 9
Name the country

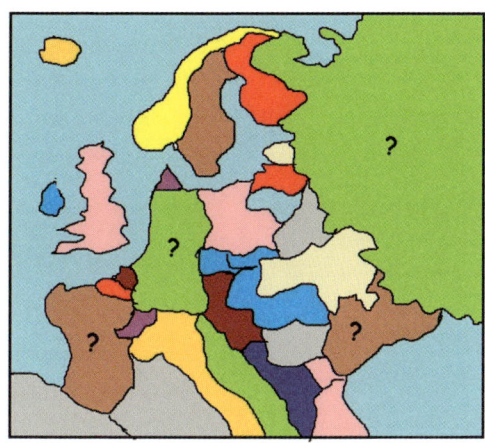

How to play the game

Teams.

Preparation: Pick teams. Toss a coin to decide who starts.

The idea of the game: To get points by correctly identifying the name of a country.

Playing the game: There are four clues as to the identity of a country. After each clue every team can have one guess. Teams can either guess immediately and hope they are correct, or they can wait until they have heard the guesses of the other teams. Both strategies carry their own risks. If the country is correctly identified after clue one, the team receives four points, after clue two three points, etc. Once a country has been identified, the points are written on the board and you move along to the next country. The team with the most points wins the game.

1. Sweden

1. Population: 9 million

2. Currency: krona

3. Word clue: tack

4. Location: Scandinavia

2. Israel

1. Population: 8 million

2. Currency: shekel

3. Word clue: shalom

4. Location: Middle East

3. Indonesia

1. Population: 238 million

2. Religion: 88% Muslim

3. Currency: rupiah

4. Capital: Jakarta

4. Greece

1. Population: 11 million

2. Currency: euro

3. Word clue: Help!

4. Capital: Athens

5. Egypt

1. Population: 82.5 million

2. Currency: pound

3. Language: Arabic

4. Capital: Cairo

6. Luxembourg

1. Population: 520,000

2. Currency: euro (used to be the Franc)

3. Languages: German, French, Luxembourgish

4. A. K. A (also known as): Grand Duchy

1. Australia

1. Population: 19.3 million

2. Independence: 1 January, 1901

3. Currency: dollar

4. Official language: English

2. Poland

1. Population: 38.6 million

2. Independence:
   11 November, 1918

3. Politics: republic

4. Currency: złoty

3. San Marino

1. The third smallest state
   in Europe

2. Population: 27,336

3. Language: Italian

4. Currency: used to be lira
   (now euro)

4. Brazil

1. Population: 174 million

2. Coastline: 7,491 km

3. Border countries:
   Argentina, Bolivia, Colombia

4. Language: Portuguese

5. Pakistan

1. Population: 144 million

2. Religion: Muslim 97%

3. Independence:
   14 August, 1947 (from UK)

4. Currency: rupee

6. Canada

1. Population: 31.5 million

2. Independence:
   1 July, 1867 (from UK)

3. Languages: English & French

4. Currency: dollar

47

Name the day

'Do you remember where you were when JR got shot?'

How to play the game

Teams.

Preparation: Photocopy the game and distribute it among the teams.

The idea of the game: To get points by stating when certain historical events took place.

Playing the game: Ask the teams to fill in the quiz stating year, month and date. (For example: 22 January, 1987.) Teams score one point for the correct year, two points for the correct year and month and five points if they have all three. The team with the most points wins the game.

Event	Date
1. Neil Armstrong walked on the moon	
2. Soviet Union's Yuri Gagarin became the first man in space	
3. The U. S. dropped the atomic bomb on Hiroshima	
4. Germany invaded Poland	
5. Live Aid	
6. Assassination of JFK	
7. England won the World Cup at Wembley	
8. Building began on the Berlin Wall	
9. The Berlin Wall came down	
10. The Beatles split	

Event	Date
1. Attack on the Twin Towers in New York	
2. The assassination of Martin Luther King	
3. The sinking of the Titanic	
4. Nelson Mandela freed from prison in South Africa	
5. Prince Charles and Princess Diana marry at Westminster Abbey	
6. The First World War ends	
7. Princess Diana dies in a car crash in Paris	
8. Concorde crashes on take-off in Paris	
9. Germany last won the World Cup	
10. Angela Merkel becomes Chancellor of Germany	

Game No. 11
Last man standing spelling game

'I wanted to hold that!'

How to play the game

Class game.

Preparation: To start the game, all the class has to stand up.

The idea of the game: To spell words correctly to stay in, and win, the game.

Playing the game: Choose a player to start the game. Choose words at random from the list and ask the players to spell them.

Each player has to give the next letter of the word. (Write down the word on the board as it's being spelt.) If a player gets the spelling wrong, they have to sit down and are out of the game. The last player standing wins the game.

Czechoslovakia	Connecticut	February	accessible
accommodate	amateur	ambidextrous	amoeba
anxious	anonymous	anecdote	entrepreneur
apparatus	apartheid	apostrophe	archaeology
aardvark	asbestos	prohibitive	pronunciation
proprietor	protein	protocol	pumpkin
queue	choir	rendezvous	rhapsody
repertoire	rapport	muscle	moustache
maestro	necessary	neutral	gnome
a cappella	satellite	receiver	psychiatrist

How old were they?

How to play the game

Teams or individuals.

Preparation: Photocopy the game and distribute it among the teams/individuals.

The idea of the game: NOT to get points! Getting as close as possible to people's ages at the time of their death in order not to score points.

Playing the game: Give the teams/individuals time to fill in the sheet. If they gets the age at the time of death correct they get zero points. Otherwise they receive a point for every year they are out. For example, if the answer is 50 and someone guesses 55, they get five points. The team/individual with the least amount of points wins the game.

Name	Age	Points
1. Juliet		
2. John Lennon		
3. JFK		
4. Marilyn Monroe		
5. Winston Churchill		
6. Freddie Mercury		
7. Michael Jackson		
8. John Wayne		
9. Karl Marx		
10. Osama Bin Laden		
	Team total:	

Name	Age	Points
1. Jimi Hendrix		
2. Amy Winehouse		
3. Janis Joplin		
4. Jim Morrison		
5. Kurt Cobain		
6. The Queen Mother		
7. James Dean		
8. Elvis Presley		
9. Frank Sinatra		
10. Princess Diana		
	Team total:	

Lateral thinking game

'Search me?'

How to play the game

Teams or individuals.

The idea of the game: To get points by working our lateral thinking posers.

Playing the game: Read out the lateral thinking posers to the teams/individuals. The players may have as many guesses as they wish to find the answer. The first team/individual to get the right answer gets a point. The most points wins the game.

Poser No. 1 – Fishy business

The police are called to a house where they find the dead bodies of Sue and Sam. The window has been broken and broken glass and a house brick are found next to the bodies. The police investigate the broken window, but make no attempt to find the killers of Sue and Sam.

Why?

Poser No. 2 – Have your cake and eat it

You must cut a birthday cake into exactly eight pieces, but you're only allowed to make three straight cuts, and you can't move pieces of the cake as you cut.

How can you do it?

Poser No. 3 – To the letter

What is the next letter in this sequence?

M   A   M   __?__

Poser No. 4 – Red-letter day

What is the next letter in this sequence?

E   F   G   __?__

Poser No. 5 – Good egg

There are six eggs in the basket.
Six people each take one of the eggs.
How can it be that one egg is left in the basket?

Poser No. 1 – Food for thought

A farmer has to cross a river to his farm in his boat. He has with him a chicken, a fox and a bag of corn. The boat will only hold the farmer and one of the other things.

How can the farmer get everything across to the other side of the river safely?

(Remember: If the farmer leaves the fox alone with the chicken, the fox will eat the chicken. If the chicken is left alone with the corn, it will eat it!)

Poser No. 2 – Next please

What is the next letter in the sequence?

D   F   S   _?_

Poser No. 3 – Follow me

What is the next letter in this sequence?

E   B   G   D   A   _?_

Poser No. 4 – A whole lot of bottle

If you put a coin in an empty bottle and insert a cork into the neck of the bottle, how could you remove the coin without taking the cork out or breaking the bottle?

Poser No. 5 – Your call

Why are there so many Müllers in the German telephone book?

Poser No. 1 – We have lift-off

A man lives on the twelfth floor of an apartment building. Every morning he takes the elevator down to the lobby and leaves the building. In the evening, he gets into the elevator, and, if there is someone else in the elevator he goes back to his floor directly. Otherwise, he goes to the tenth floor and walks up two flights of stairs to his apartment.

Why?

Poser No. 2 – Wet feet?

A man is found hanging in an otherwise empty, locked room with a puddle of water under his feet.

Where did the water come from?

Poser No. 3 – Good shot

A woman shoots her husband. Then she holds him under water for over five minutes. Finally, she hangs him. But five minutes later they both go out together and enjoy a wonderful dinner together. How is this possible?

Poser No. 4 – Happy days

Can you name three consecutive days without using the words Monday, Tuesday, Wednesday, Thursday, Friday, Saturday, or Sunday?

Poser No. 5 – Burn in hell

A man is sent to hell. When he arrives, he has to choose between three rooms. The first is full of raging fires, the second is full of assassins with loaded guns, and the third is full of lions that haven't eaten in three years. Which room is safest for him?

Game No. 14
Name the other half

'Does my mouth look big in this dress?'

How to play the game

Teams or individuals.

Preparation: Pick two teams, decide how many rounds there will be.

The idea of the game: To get points by working out the other half of famous pairs

Playing the game: In each round, teams/individuals may choose an easy question got one point, a medium question for two points or a hard question for three points. If they give an incorrect answer, the other teams/individuals may answer the question to get bonus points. The first team/individual to shout out the correct answer gets the bonus points. Only one guess per team/individual is allowed. The most points wins the game.

Easy (one point)	Medium (two points)	Difficult (three points)
Romeo (Shakespeare play)	Abbott (early film stars)	Alabama (cocktail)
Laurel (early movie stars)	Antony (Shakespeare play)	Bread (an English pudding)
Adam (first man & woman)	Lake (region in England)	Act (Beatles song)
Napoleon (French leader)	Get (Beatles song)	Great (seaside town in GB)
Bonnie (gangsters)	Land's (place in England)	Lovely (Beatles song)
Sherlock Holmes (detective)	Nowhere (Beatles song)	Snow- (cocktail)
Heavy (type of music)	Man- (cocktail)	Atlantic (Rod Stewart LP)
Dr Jekyll (monsters)	Nowhere (Beatles song)	New (region in England)
Simon (singers)	New- (English city)	Mid- (region in England)
Acid (type of music)	Monte (city)	Fame (English idiom)
Bloody (cocktail)	Thrash (type of music)	Easy (type of music)
Bucks (cocktail)	Rag- (type of music)	Corpse (cocktail)
Eleanor (Beatles song)	Torvill (ice-skaters)	Dirt (English expression)
Paperback (Beatles song)	Wallace (cartoon characters)	Bone (American insult)
Man- (English city)	Wait (English idiom)	Bangers (English dish)
Great (film)	Catch (famous book)	Chalk (English idiom)
New (Indian city)	Black (spider)	Rocka- (type of music)
Corn (English county)	The Black (plague)	Mills (publisher)
Stone (famous sight)	Big (financial term)	Death- (beetle)
Hip (type of music)	Half Man (group)	Uriah (rock group)
Free (type of music)	Kama (sex book)	Bubble (English dish)

Who's telling the truth?

It wasn't me!

How to play the game

Team game for teams each with three players or more.

Preparation: Photocopy and cut out the individual cards.

The idea of the game: To get points by working out who is telling the truth.

Playing the game: Distribute three cards to one team. Each card contains 'a fact' about a well-known person, but only one of them is true. Each team member reads out his/her fact. The other team have to guess who's telling the truth?' Teams get a point for each correct guess. The most points wins the game.

Who's telling the truth?	Who's telling the truth?	Who's telling the truth?
1. Tom Cruise	**1. Tom Cruise**	**1. Tom Cruise**
Trained to be a pilot	Trained to be a dentist	Trained to be a priest
FALSE	**FALSE**	**TRUE**
Who's telling the truth?	Who's telling the truth?	Who's telling the truth?
2. Charlie Chaplin	**2. Charlie Chaplin**	**2. Charlie Chaplin**
Once won third prize in a yodelling contest	Once won third prize in a Charlie Chaplin lookalike contest	Once won third prize in a Mr Universe contest
FALSE	**TRUE**	**FALSE**
Who's telling the truth?	Who's telling the truth?	Who's telling the truth?
3. Brad Pitt	**3. Brad Pitt**	**3. Brad Pitt**
Once worked as a chauffeur	Once worked as a bus driver	Once worked as a taxi driver
TRUE	**FALSE**	**FALSE**
Who's telling the truth?	Who's telling the truth?	Who's telling the truth?
4. Keanu Reeves	**4. Keanu Reeves**	**4. Keanu Reeves**
Is afraid of mice	Is afraid of the dark	Is afraid of dogs
FALSE	**TRUE**	**FALSE**
Who's telling the truth?	Who's telling the truth?	Who's telling the truth?
5. Leonardo da Vinci	**5. Leonardo da Vinci**	**5. Leonardo da Vinci**
Invented the scissors	Invented the stapler	Invented the iron
TRUE	**FALSE**	**FALSE**

Who's telling the truth?	Who's telling the truth?	Who's telling the truth?
6. Pierce Brosnan	**6. Pierce Brosnan**	**6. Pierce Brosnan**
Worked in the circus as a ringmaster	Worked in the circus as a lion tamer	Worked in the circus as a fire eater
FALSE	**FALSE**	**TRUE**
Who's telling the truth?	Who's telling the truth?	Who's telling the truth?
7. Rod Stewart	**7. Rod Stewart**	**7. Rod Stewart**
One of his first jobs was as a gravedigger	One of his first jobs was as a footballer	One of his first jobs was as a DJ
TRUE	**FALSE**	**FALSE**
Who's telling the truth?	Who's telling the truth?	Who's telling the truth?
8. Madonna	**8. Madonna**	**8. Madonna**
Used to work at Dunkin' Donuts	Used to work at Burger King	Used to work at Kentucky Fried Chicken
TRUE	**FALSE**	**FALSE**
Who's telling the truth?	Who's telling the truth?	Who's telling the truth?
9. Sean Connery	**9. Sean Connery**	**9. Sean Connery**
Used to be a coal miner	Used to be a dustman	Used to be a road sweeper
FALSE	**TRUE**	**FALSE**
Who's telling the truth?	Who's telling the truth?	Who's telling the truth?
10. Mel Gibson	**10. Mel Gibson**	**10. Mel Gibson**
Was discovered whilst working as a hairdresser	Was discovered whilst working as a window cleaner	Was discovered whilst working as a carwash
TRUE	**FALSE**	**FALSE**

Who's telling the truth?	Who's telling the truth?	Who's telling the truth?
1. Mick Jagger	**1. Mick Jagger**	**1. Mick Jagger**
Used to work in a mental hospital	Used to work in an old folks' home	Used to work in a library
TRUE	**FALSE**	**FALSE**

Who's telling the truth?	Who's telling the truth?	Who's telling the truth?
2. John Paul Getty	**2. John Paul Getty**	**2. John Paul Getty**
Had a payphone in his mansion	Had a parking meter outside his mansion	Had a lock on his fridge in his mansion
TRUE	**FALSE**	**FALSE**

Who's telling the truth?	Who's telling the truth?	Who's telling the truth?
3. David Beckham	**3. David Beckham**	**3. David Beckham**
Victoria Beckham's nickname for her husband is 'golden babe'	Victoria Beckham's nickname for her husband is 'golden boy'	Victoria Beckham's nickname for her husband is 'golden balls'
FALSE	**FALSE**	**TRUE**

Who's telling the truth?	Who's telling the truth?	Who's telling the truth?
4. Elvis Presley	**4. Elvis Presley**	**4. Elvis Presley**
Wrote most of his own songs	Never recorded any of his own songs	Wrote all his own songs
FALSE	**TRUE**	**FALSE**

Who's telling the truth?	Who's telling the truth?	Who's telling the truth?
5. Fidel Castro	**5. Fidel Castro**	**5. Fidel Castro**
Has appeared in two Hollywood films	Has appeared in a fast food commercial	Recorded an album of folk songs
TRUE	**FALSE**	**FALSE**

Who's telling the truth?	Who's telling the truth?	Who's telling the truth?
6. Al Capone	**6. Al Capone**	**6. Al Capone**
His business card said he was a second hand car salesman	His business card said he was a brush salesman	His business card said he was a second hand furniture salesman
FALSE	**FALSE**	**TRUE**

Who's telling the truth?	Who's telling the truth?	Who's telling the truth?
7. Prince Charles	**7. Prince Charles**	**7. Prince Charles**
Is a trained helicopter pilot	Is a trained fighter jet pilot	Is a trained glider pilot
TRUE	**FALSE**	**FALSE**

Who's telling the truth?	Who's telling the truth?	Who's telling the truth?
8. Yasser Arafat	**8. Yasser Arafat**	**8. Yasser Arafat**
Won an Olympic gold medal	Won the Nobel Peace Prize	Played in the World Cup for Palestine
FALSE	**TRUE**	**FALSE**

Who's telling the truth?	Who's telling the truth?	Who's telling the truth?
9. Def Leppard	**9. Def Leppard**	**9. Def Leppard**
The Def Leppard drummer only has one leg	The Def Leppard drummer only has one arm	The Def Leppard drummer only has one eye
FALSE	**TRUE**	**FALSE**

Who's telling the truth?	Who's telling the truth?	Who's telling the truth?
10. Sean Connery	**10. Sean Connery**	**10. Sean Connery**
Wore a toupee in every Bond film he made	Wore a corset in every Bond film he made	Wore women's panties in every Bond film he made
TRUE	**FALSE**	**FALSE**

Firsts quiz

I was here first!

How to play the game

Teams/individuals.

The idea of the game: To get points by using clues to find the answers to the questions.

Playing the game: Each round has five clues as to the identity of 'a first'. Teams/individuals get five points if they guess the answer after clue one, four points after clue two, and so on. Read out a clue. Each team/individual can have one guess. They can either guess immediately, or wait until they hear the other answers. Both strategies are risky. The team/individual with the most points after question six wins the game.

Question 1

1. What was the first product to use a barcode?

2. It comes in a packet

3. It is classified under 'sweets'

4. You put it in your mouth, but you don't swallow it

5. Wrigley's

Question 2

1. Sally Ride was the first American woman to do what?

2. Major Tom

3. NASA

4. Rocket man

5. Space cowgirl

Question 3

1. Paul Tibbets was the first man to do what?

2. Enola Gay

3. Hiroshima

4. 1941

5. Japan – 'War! What is it good for? Absolutely nothing!'

Question 4

1. 'Mr. Watson, come here, I want to see you.' were the first words spoken on what?

2. Dog & bone

3. Telecommunications

4. Very handy

5. Alexander Graham Bell

Question 5

1. 'Wait a minute, wait a minute, you ain't heard nothin' yet!' were the first words spoken where?

2. The Jazz Singer

3. Hollywood

4. Cinema

5. Popcorn

Question 6

1. Richard Nixon was the first American president to do what?

2. All The President's Men (Die Unbestechlichen)

3. Watergate

4. Burglary

5. Lies

Who is it?

Is it me?

How to play the game

Teams/individuals.

The idea of the game: To get points by using clues to identify famous people.

Playing the game: Each round has five clues as to the identity of a famous person. Teams/individuals get five points if they get the correct answer after question one, four points after question two, and so on. Read out a clue. Each team/individual can have one guess. They can either guess immediately, or wait until they hear the other answers. Both strategies are risky. The team/individual with the most points after subject 10 wins the game.

Subject 1
1. The army
2. Health care
3. Honolulu or Kenya?
4. Second term
5. US president

Subject 2
1. Schnapps
2. Boy band
3. Millenium
4. Angels
5. Take That

Subject 3
1. The Rolling Stones
2. Hamburg
3. First woman
4. CDU
5. Politics

Subject 4
1. Tokyo
2. Peace
3. Oh no!
4. Imagine
5. John Lennon

Subject 5
1. The State Lottery
2. Still Life
3. Self-portrait
4. Wheat Field
5. Sunflowers

Subject 6
1. M
2. Q
3. I-Spy
4. Sean Connery
5. Pierce Brosnan

Subject 7
1. Rechnung
2. Tore
3. Fenster
4. Microsoft
5. Computer

Subject 8
1. Monty Python
2. The Life of Brian
3. Cross
4. The Bible
5. Son of God

Subject 9
1. Cowboy hat
2. Initials
3. Oil
4. Dallas
5. Larry

Subject 10
1. America
2. Italian? Portuguese?
3. Discovery
4. Sailor
5. Boats

Game No. 18
Opposites

'But it's true! We are like chalk and cheese!'

How to play the game

Teams.

Preparation: Select teams. Write the team names down on the board. Decide how many rounds the game will have (usually three). Toss a coin to decide which team starts.

The idea of the game: To get points by naming opposites.

Playing the game: Read out a word from the left hand column. Teams get a point when they correctly name the opposite of that word. Say the running total aloud after each correct answer. When the teams think they have enough points, they can 'bank' their points. The total is then written on the board and added to the team's total. A team must say 'bank' before they hear the next word. If a team doesn't 'bank' their points and gives an incorrect answer or does not know the answer, all the points from that round are lost. A round is over when a team banks their points, gives an incorrect answer or is unable to give an answer. The team with the most points wins the game.

about	exactly	certainly	probably
above	below	changeable	constant
absence	presence	cheap	expensive
abundance	lack	child	adult, grown-up
(to) accept	(to) refuse	children	parents
accidental	intentional	clean	dirty
active	lazy	clear	cloudy
(to) add	(to) subtract	clever	stupid
(to) admit	(to) deny	(to) close	(to) open
adult	child	closed	open
advanced	elementary	cloudy	clear, sunny, bright
affirmative	negative	(to) destroy	(to) build, (to) create
afraid	brave	destruction	construction
after	before	devil	God
against	for	dictatorship	republic
alike	different	(to) die	(to) live
back	front	different	alike, the same
background	foreground	difficult	easy
backward	forward	disease	health
bad	good	distant	near
bad luck	good luck	(to) divide	(to) unite
beauty	ugliness	division	unity
(to) begin	(to) end, (to) stop	(to) divorce	(to) marry
beginning	end, ending	divorce	marriage, wedding
behind	in front of	divorced	married
best	worst	domestic	foreign
better	worse	down	up
beautiful	ugly	downstairs	upstairs
break	fix, mend, repair	early	late
calm	excited	east	west
careful	careless	easy	difficult, hard
(to) catch	(to) throw	elementary	advanced
ceiling	floor	(to) emigrate	(to) immigrate
cellar	attic	emigration	immigration
centre	outskirts, suburb	empty	full

(to) end	(to) begin	generous	mean
end	beginning	gentle	violent, rough
ending	beginning	gentleman	lady
enemy	friend	girl	boy
(to) enjoy	(to) hate	(to) give	(to) take
(to) enter	(to) leave	(to) go	(to) come, (to) stop
entrance	exit	good	bad
equal	different	grown-up	child
even	odd	guest	host
evening	morning	guilty	innocent
everybody	nobody	happiness	sadness
everything	nothing	happy	sad
exactly	about, approximately	handsome	ugly
excited	calm	hard	easy, soft
exciting	boring	(to) harvest	(to) plant
(to) finish	(to) begin	(to) hate	(to) enjoy, (to) like, (to) love
finish	start		
first	final, last	health	disease, illness
(to) fix	(to) break	healthy	ill, sick
flat	hilly	heat	cold
floor	ceiling	heaven	hell
(to) follow	(to) lead	heavy	light
(to) forbid	(to) allow, (to) permit	hell	heaven
for	against	here	there
foreground	background	high	deep
foreign	domestic	high	low
foreigner	native	in front of	back, behind
(to) forget	(to) remember	(to) ignore	(to) notice
(to) form	(to) destroy	ill	healthy, well
fortune	bad luck	(to) immigrate	(to) emigrate
forward	backward		
(to) free	(to) arrest, (to) capture	immigration	emigration
(to) freeze	(to) melt	import	export
funny	serious	in	out
general	particular, special	(to) include	(to) exclude

(to) increase	(to) reduce	nephew	niece
innocent	guilty	never	always
inside	outside	nice	awful, nasty
insult	compliment	niece	nephew
intelligent	silly, stupid	night	day
intentional	accidental	no	yes
interesting	boring, dull	nobody	everybody
junior	senior	noisy	quiet, silent
kind	cruel	noon	midnight
lack	abundance, plenty	none	a lot of
lady	gentleman	north	south
(to) land	(to) take off	not yet	already
land	water	nothing	everything
large	small	(to) notice	(to) ignore
last	first	now	then
major	minor	occupied	vacant
male	female	odd	even
man	woman	off	on
many	few, some	often	seldom, sometimes
marriage	divorce	old	modern, new, young
married	divorced, single	north	south
(to) marry	(to) divorce	open	closed, shut
master	servant	opponent	supporter
maximum	minimum	opposite	synonym
mean	generous	order	mess
(to) melt	(to) freeze	ordinary	special
men	women	other	same
(to) mend	(to) break	out	in
mess	order	outside	inside
narrow	broad, wide	outskirts	centre
nasty	nice, pleasant	over	under
native	foreigner, stranger	parents	children
natural	artificial	part	whole
near	distant, far	partial	total
negative	affirmative	particular	general

(to) pass	(to) fail	(to) reply	(to) ask
past	future, present	reply	question
peace	war	republic	dictatorship, monarchy
(to) permit	(to) allow, (to) forbid	(to) rest	(to) work
(to) plant	(to) harvest	right	left, wrong
plenty	lack	(to) rise	(to) sink
pleasant	awful	rough	gentle, smooth, soft
polite	rude	rude	polite
poor	rich, wealthy	rural	urban
poverty	wealth	sad	happy
powerful	weak	sadness	happiness
presence	absence	safe	dangerous
present	past, future	safety	danger
pretty	ugly	salt	sugar
private	public	(the) same	different, the other
probably	certainly	sane	insane, crazy
professional	amateur	simple	complicated
(to) protect	(to) attack	(to) save	(to) spend, (to) waste
protection	attack	(to) scream	(to) whisper
public	private	security	danger
(to) pull	(to) push	seldom	often
pupil	teacher	(to) sell	(to) buy
(to) push	(to) pull	(to) send	(to) receive
question	answer	senior	junior
quick	slow	(to) separate	(to) connect, (to) unite
quiet	loud, noisy	serious	funny
(to) raise	(to) lower	(to) take	(to) give
rainy	sunny	(to) take off	(to) land
rear	front	tall	small, short
(to) receive	(to) send	(to) teach	(to) learn
(to) reduce	(to) increase	teacher	pupil, student
(to) refuse	(to) agree, (to) accept	then	now
regret	satisfaction	terrible	lovely, great
(to) remember	(to) forget	there	here
(to) repair	(to) damage	thick	thin

thin	thick, fat	wake	fall asleep
thirsty	hungry	warm	cool
(to) throw	(to) catch	(to) waste	(to) save
tight	loose	water	land
tiny	huge	weak	powerful, strong
together	apart	wealth	poverty
tomorrow	yesterday	wealthy	poor
top	bottom	wedding	divorce
total	partial	welcome	unwelcome
town	village	well	ill
tragedy	comedy	west	east
true	false	wet	dry
(to) trust	(to) suspect	(to) whisper	(to) scream, (to) shout
ugliness	beauty	white	black
ugly	beautiful, handsome (boys), pretty (girls)	whole	part
		wide	narrow
understood	misunderstood	wife	husband
unruly	quiet	(to) win	(to) lose
unschooled	educated	willing	unwilling
(to) unite	(to) divide, (to) separate	wild	tame, domesticated
unity	division	will	won't
up	down	with	without
upstairs	downstairs	winner	loser
urban	rural	wise	dumb, stupid
useful	useless	winter	summer
useless	useful	(to) work	(to) rest
vacant	occupied	whole	part, partly
valley	mountain	woman	man
vertical	horizontal	wonderful	awful, terrible
victory	defeat	work	rest
village	town	worse	better
violent	gentle	worst	best
visitor	host	wrong	correct, right
voluntary	compulsory	yesterday	tomorrow
war	peace	young	old

Crazy headlines game

CLASSROOM GAMES BOOK SELLS TWO MILLION COPIES!

How to play the game

Teams/individuals.

Preparation: Photocopy the game and distribute it among the teams/individuals.

The idea of the game: To guess the missing words in newspaper headlines.

Playing the game: Give the teams/individuals time to study the sheet and come up with answers. Award three points for a correct answer, two points for a very close answer and one point if an answer makes the class laugh! Write down the scores on the board after each round. The team/individual with the most points wins the game.

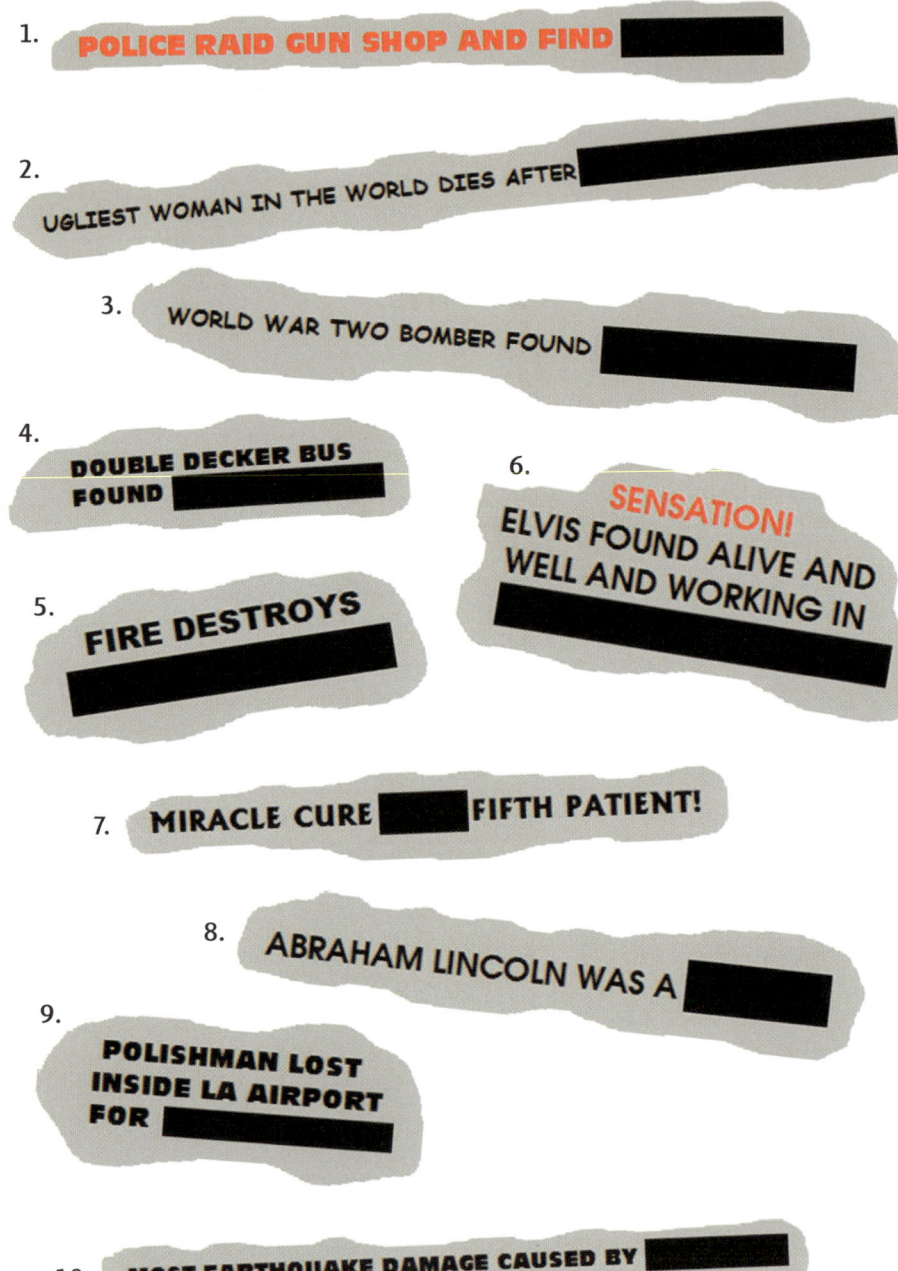

1. POLICE RAID GUN SHOP AND FIND

2. UGLIEST WOMAN IN THE WORLD DIES AFTER

3. WORLD WAR TWO BOMBER FOUND

4. DOUBLE DECKER BUS FOUND

6. SENSATION!
ELVIS FOUND ALIVE AND WELL AND WORKING IN

5. FIRE DESTROYS

7. MIRACLE CURE   FIFTH PATIENT!

8. ABRAHAM LINCOLN WAS A

9. POLISHMAN LOST INSIDE LA AIRPORT FOR

10. MOST EARTHQUAKE DAMAGE CAUSED BY

76

Game No. 20
Quotes of the rich and famous

'Of course I'd like to be as thin as those African kids, but without all the flies and stuff!' (Mariah Carey)

How to play the game

Teams.

Preparation: Pick two or more teams. Photocopy the game and distribute it among the teams.

The idea of the game: To guess the missing words of famous quotes.

Playing the game: Give the teams time to discuss and write down their answers. Award three points for a correct answer, two points for a very close answer and one point if an answer makes the class laugh! Write down the scores on the board after each round. The team with the most points wins the game.

No. 1

> Be good. And if you can't be good, be _____

Mae West
50s film star

No. 2

> Life is too short to _____

Oscar Wilde
Irish poet and writer

> We are more popular than _____

No. 3

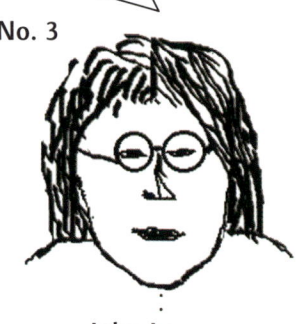

> I spent 90% of my money on women, champagne and fast cars, the rest I just _____

No. 4

John Lennon
Beatle

George Best
Britain's first 'pop star' footballer

No. 5

> Girls, don't get mad – get _____

Ivana Trump
Ex-wife of American billionaire
Donald Trump

Winston Churchill
Former Prime Minister

No. 1

You can always count on the Americans to do the right thing

_____

I never forget a face, but in your case I will

_____

No. 2

I owe a lot to my parents, especially

_____

No. 3

Groucho Marx
Film star & comedian

George W. Bush
Former US president

And how long have you had this

_____

on air

No. 4

BBC Radio One DJ

Whenever I can, I always watch the Detroit Tigers on the _____

No. 5

Gerald Ford
Former US president

Find the connection game

'So Mr Jenkins, you still believe that your weight problems have got no connection whatsoever with drinking beer?'

How to play the game

Teams.

Preparation: Pick two teams. Toss a coin to decide which team starts.

The idea of the game: To get points by finding the connection between three different words/people/ objects, etc.

Playing the game: Write the three words on the board. The first team to find the connection gets the points indicated in brackets. Teams may have as many guesses as they like. *The teacher may give clues for the harder questions.* Write down the points on the board after each correct answer. The team with the most points wins the game.

1. saber-toothed tiger	mammoth	dinosaur **(one point)**
2. die	boot	tag **(five points)**
3. Simply Red	Pink Floyd	Black Sabbath **(one point)**
4. Paul McCartney	Jimmy Hendrix	Napoleon **(two points)**
5. George Lazenby	Pierce Brosnan	Roger Moore **(one point)**
6. John Lennon	John F. Kennedy	Ronald Reagan **(two points)**
7. moon	velvet	berry hill **(five points)**
8. civic	deed	madam **(two points)**
9. now	night	not **(five points)**
10. read	write	wait **(five points)**
11. I Don't Want To Talk About It Rod Stewart	Careless Whisper George Michael	Shout Tears for Fears **(two points)**
12. drink	eat	drive **(two points)**
13. fast	hard	early **(five points)**
14. Thunderbird	Jaguar	Mustang **(three points)**
15. David	Hugh	Bob **(three points)**

1. Christopher Robin	Eeyore	Piglet **(one point)**
2. The Lion King	Cats	Beauty and the Beast **(two points)**
3. Queen's Park	Victoria	Seven Sisters **(six points)**
4. The Eagles	Cat Stevens	Boomtown Rats **(one point)**
5. scissors	parachute	high heels **(two points)**
6. Uranus	Neptune	Pluto **(six points)**
7. e-mail	post	hand **(five points)**
8. dancing	gown	blitz **(five points)**
9. bread	forward	rock and **(three points)**
10. Barack Obama	Bill Clinton	Ronald Reagan **(five points)**
11. Ukraine	Belarus	Latvia **(two points)**
12. Hyde	Regent's	Green **(two points)**
13. Lionel Richie	The Monkees	Def Leppard **(one point)**
14. Red Hot Chilli Peppers	Bread	Meatloaf **(two points)**
15. daisies	chrysanthemums	sunflowers **(six points)**

Noughts & crosses trivia game

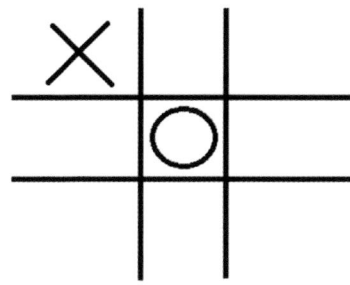

How to play the game

Teams.

Preparation: Pick two teams. Draw a noughts and crosses grid on the board. Pick two teams and a team captain for each. Decide how many points wins the game.

The idea of the game: To get three noughts or crosses in a line to get a point.

Playing the game: Toss a coin to decide which teams starts. Pick a trivia question at random from the list. The teams may discuss their answers, but you take the final answer from the team captain only. Set a time limit for each question. (Between 20–30 seconds.) If a team answers correctly, they may place their nought or cross anywhere on the grid. A team is not only attempting to get three noughts or crosses in a row, but also trying to prevent the opposing team from getting three in a row. A team which gets three noughts or crosses in a line gets a point. The team which reaches the agreed winning total first wins the game.

Art and Literature

Who lived at 221B, Baker Street, London? (Sherlock Holmes)

Who cut off Van Gogh's ear? (He did it himself.)

Who wrote the James Bond books? (Ian Fleming)

Who painted the Mona Lisa? (Da Vinci)

What did the crocodile swallow in Peter Pan? (An alarm clock)

Who painted the Sistine Chapel? (Michelangelo)

Entertainment

What year did Elvis Presley die? (1977)

Name two actors who have played James Bond. (Sean Connery, George Lazenby, Timothy Dalton, Pierce Brosnan, Roger Moore, Daniel Craig)

Who was the director of the film 'Psycho'? (Alfred Hitchcock)

In which city is Hollywood? (Los Angeles)

Geography

What's the smallest country in the world? (Vatican City)

What is the capital of Australia? (Canberra)

What's the largest city in India? (Bombay)

What's the capital of Denmark? (Copenhagen)

What's the capital of Brazil? (Brasilia)

Which river goes through London? (Thames)

What's the highest mountain in Africa? (Kilimanjaro)

What's the capital of Finland? (Helsinki)

History

How many wives did Henry the Eighth have? (six)

When did the first man go into space? (1961)

Who was the first man on the moon? (Neil Armstrong)

When was President Kennedy killed? (1963)

Sport and Leisure

What British sport do you associate with the terms Silly Mid On, Short Square Leg, Slip and Gully? (Cricket)

Which member of the British Royal family has competed at the Olympic Games? (Princess Anne)

How many players are there in a basketball team? (5)

How many squares are there on a chess board? (64)

How many events are there in the decathlon? (10)

How many players are there in a volleyball team? (6)

Science and Nature

How many colours are there in a rainbow? (7)

How many legs has a spider got? (8)

What temperature does water boil at? (100 °C)

Which planet is nearest the sun? (Mercury)

What colours make purple? (Red and blue)

What's the hardest rock? (Diamond)

How much does a litre of water weigh? (1 kg)

Who wants to be an (English) millionaire?

How to play the game

Teams/individuals.

Preparation: Photocopy the game and distribute it among the teams/individuals.

The idea of the game: To be the last one left, thus winning the game.

Playing the game: Each team/individual must answer the questions by underlining their answers. If they have the correct answer, they move onto the next round. If they have chosen an incorrect answer, they are out of the game. The last team/individual left in the game wins.

Lifelines: Each team/individual has two lifelines. If they use the '50:50' lifeline, the teacher crosses out two incorrect answers on their sheet. If they use the 'ask the teacher' lifeline, the teacher underlines an answer on their sheet. *(Explain to the class that the teacher is not obliged to underline the correct answer!)*

Tiebreaker: In the event of two or more teams/individuals still being in the game after question 10, the tiebreaker comes into play. The first team/individual to put the cities in the correct order wins the game.

Question 1
Where does the Queen live?

a. Buckingham Palace	b. Downing Street
c. Windsor Castle	d. Balmoral Castle

Question 2
Who lives at 10 Downing Street?

a. Prince Charles	b. Prince Edward
c. Prime Minister	d. Prince Harry

Question 3
Which river flows through London?

a. The Nile	b. The Thames
c. The Avon	d. The Amazon

Question 4
The Beatles came from which famous English city?

a. Liverpool	b. Manchester
c. London	d. Birmingham

Question 5
Wimbledon in London is famous for what?

a. Cricket	b. Tennis
c. Football	d. Boxing

Question 6

Where are the crown jewels kept?

a. Windsor Castle	b. Buckingham Palace
c. Tower of London	d. Wembley Stadium

Question 7

Who married Prince Charles?

a. Pricilla Presley	b. Camilla Parker-Bowles
c. Mariah Carey	d. Prince Harry

Question 8

How old must someone be in Britain to vote?

a. 18	b. 21
c. 16	d. 25

Question 9

How old must someone be in Britain to buy alcohol?

a. 16	b. 17
c. 18	d. 21

Question 10

Margaret Thatcher was the leader of which political party?

a. The Labour Party	b. The Monster Raving Loony Party
c. The Conservative Party	d. The Communist Party

Tiebreaker

Put the following British cities in order from north to south:

Glasgow   Birmingham   Manchester   Portsmouth

The choice is yours

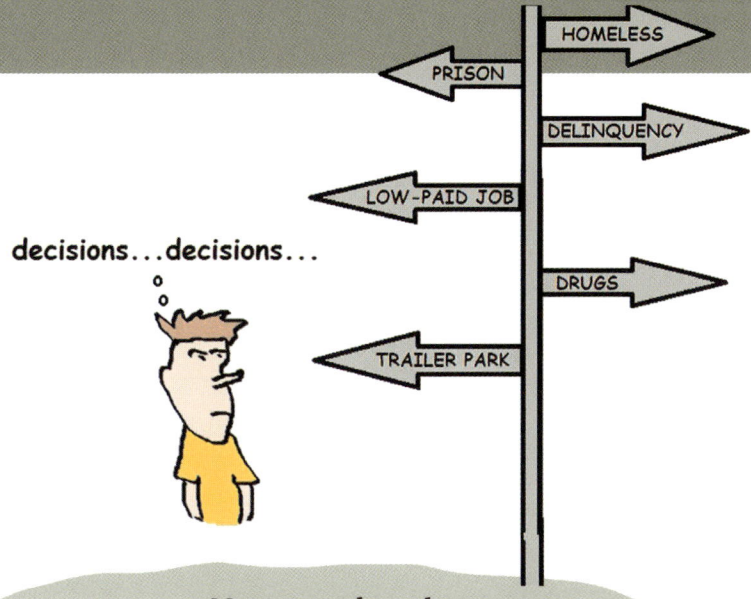

decisions...decisions...

HOMELESS

PRISON

DELINQUENCY

LOW-PAID JOB

DRUGS

TRAILER PARK

How to play the game

Teams.

Preparation: Photocopy the game and give each team member a copy.

The idea of the game: To get points by guessing your opponent's preferences.

Playing the game: Each player is given a member of the other team as their personal 'opponent'. The players fill in their own preferences on the sheet, then they have try to guess their personal opponent's answers. Teams then take it in turn to read out their guesses and their personal opponent must answer either 'right' or 'wrong'. (Players are not allowed to change their answers and may only refer to the answers they have written down on the sheet.)

A team gets a point for every correct answer. The team with the most points wins the game.

	You	Your opponent
1. Sparkling or still water?		
2. Bus or train?		
3. Boiled or fried egg?		
4. Ironing or vacuuming?		
5. Love story or thriller?		
6. Lawn mowing or weeding?		
7. Doing English homework or visiting your in-laws?		
8. Cleaning the oven or doing the shopping?		
9. Jogging or swimming?		
10. Changing the baby's nappy or cleaning the dustbin?		
11. Learning English vocabulary or English grammar?		
12. Speaking English on the telephone or writing an e-mail in English?		
13. Hammock or sunlounger?		
14. Bath or shower?		
15. Cocktail or spirit?		
Your score:		

	You	Your opponent
1. Wellness hotel or shopping trip?		
2. Brewery or Italian restaurant?		
3. Flowers or chocolates?		
4. Snow or sunshine?		
5. Hiking or biking?		
6. Pop concert or musical?		
7. Computer game or board game?		
8. Log fire or central heating?		
9. Surfing in the sea or on the internet?		
10. Popcorn or ice-cream?		
11. Rice or noodles?		
12. Lift or stairs?		
13. Male or female boss?		
14. Open plan or small office?		
15. TV news or game show?		
Your score:		

	You	Your opponent
1. Mobile phone or iPad?		
2. DVD or cinema?		
3. An extra day's holiday or the money?		
4. Cross country or downhill skiing?		
5. Aisle or window seat in plane?		
6. Carnival or Christmas?		
7. Newspaper or internet news?		
8. World Cup or Olympic Games?		
9. London or Paris?		
10. New York or Tokyo?		
11. Cats or dogs?		
12. Nephew or niece?		
13. Mouse or spider?		
14. Too hot or too cold?		
15. Piano or guitar?		
Your score:		

Game No. 25
It's in this room – what is it?

'Errr, one? Mobile phone?
iPad? Smart phone?
Headphones?
Laptop? Xbox?'

How to play the game

Teams/individuals.

Preparation: This is a game you must prepare during the lesson. While the students are working, make a mental note of how many people are in the room, how many men and women there are and what they are wearing, hair colour, wedding rings, glasses, etc.

The idea of the game: To get points by answering the question: 'It's in this room, what is it?'

Playing the game: Examples: 'There is one of these in this room.'

Possible answers: one teacher, one English person, one French woman, one person wearing glasses, one bald person.

Other variations: 'There are 18 of these in this room, but you can only see 16 of them.' Answer: eyes

'There are 80 of them in this room, but you can't see any of them.' Answer: toes

Teams/individuals can have as many guesses as they like. The one who gets the answer correct gets a point. The team/individual with the most points wins the game.

**'There is one of these
in this room, what is it?'**

Possible answers:
– Teacher
– Englishman/woman
– A person wearing glasses
– A man/woman wearing glasses
– Someone wearing a dress/suit/tie/
  necklace/T-shirt

**'There are ＿＿ in this room,
but you can only see ＿＿ of them.'**

Possible answers:
– Eyes
– Eyebrows
– Foreheads

**'There are ＿＿ of these in the room,
but you can't see any of them.'**

Possible answers:
– Toes
– Feet
– Hearts
– Lungs
– Brains

**Other items
which might be visible:**
– Handbags
– Mobile phones
– Pictures on the wall
– Windows
– Doors
– Books
– Laptops
– Pens/pencils
– Rubbers
– Briefcases
– Newspapers/magazines
– Keys/keyrings
– Wedding rings
– Watches

Nationalities quiz

How to play the game

Teams.

The idea of the game: To get points by naming nationalities.

Playing the game: Pick teams, set a time limit for the end of the game and toss a coin to decide who starts. A team may choose a one point, two point or three point question. Pick a country at random from the list, if a team can name the nationality of that country, they get the points.

The team with the most points wins the game.

(Easy) One point	
France	French
Pakistan	Pakistani
India	Indian
Denmark	Danish
Scotland	Scottish
Switzerland	Swiss
Greece	Greek
Hungary	Hungarian
Italy	Italian
Jamaica	ajamaican
Ireland	Irish
Spain	Spanish

Brazil	Brazilian
Canada	Canadian
Poland	Polish
Norway	Norwegian
Sweden	Swedish
Wales	Welsh
Finland	Finnish
Egypt	Egyptian
Albania	Albanian
Serbia	Serbian
Chile	Chilean
Bolivia	Bolivian
Germany	German

(Medium) Two points	
Tunisia	Tunisian
Holland	Dutch
Kenya	Kenyan
Korea	Korean
Israel	Israeli
Lybia	Libyan

Kuwait	Kuwaiti
Algeria	Algerian
Croatia	Croatian
Lebanon	Lebanese
Ethiopia	Ethiopian
Czech Rep	Czech
Singapore	Singaporean

Georgia	Georgian	Bahrain	Bahraini
Gambia	Gambian	Bulgaria	Bulgarian
Congo	Congolese	Nepal	Nepalese
Costa Rica	Costa Rican	Namibia	Namibian
Azerbaijan	Azerbaijani	Panama	Panamanian
Angola	Angolan	Paraguay	Paraguayan

(Hard) Three points			
Uruguay	Uruguayan	Cameroon	Cameroonian
Malta	Maltese	Falkland Islands	Falkland Islander
Afghanistan	Afghan	Virgin Islands	Virgin Islander
Peru	Peruvian	Burma	Burmese
Iceland	Icelandic	Bangladesh	Bangladeshi
Nicaragua	Nicaraguan	Barbados	Barbadian
Belgium	Belgian	Zimbabwe	Zimbabwean
Vietnam	Vietnamese	Senegal	Senegalese
Venezuela	Venezuelan	Oman	Omani
Trinidad	Trinidadian	Honduras	Honduran
New Zealand	New Zealander	Sudan	Sudanese
Fiji	Fijian	Mongolia	Mongolian
		Moldova	Moldovan

Game No. 27

Percentages game

How to play the game

Teams/individuals.

The idea of the game: To get points by guessing percentages.

Playing the game: Photocopy the sheets and distribute them among the teams/individuals.

Game 1

A team/individual gets one point for a correct answer or three points if they are the only ones with the correct answer.

Game 2

A team/individual get three points for a correct answer. If no one has the correct answer, the team/individual which is closest gets one point. The team/individual with the most points wins the game.

Questions	Answers

1. 29% of men and 16% of women admit to doing this in the shower.   _____

2. 47% of men and 32% of women have admitted to doing this in their cars in the last twelve months.   _____

3. 32% of women, but only 8% of men say they do this on holiday.   _____

4. 33% of men and 32% of women say they have done this in a shop in the last five years.   _____

5. 51% of women over 50 and 32% of men over 50 say they do this on a regular basis.   _____

6. Over 50% of both men and women say they never do this in a restaurant.   _____

7. 35% of married men, but only 5% of married women say they have done this within the last 10 years.   _____

8. 64% of women and 34% of men say they would never do this on a beach.   _____

9. 37% of women and 39% of men say they have done this in the sea.   _____

10. 16% of women and 19% of men say, if they could have their time again, they wouldn't do this.   _____

1. Japan has ____% of the active volcanoes in the world.

2. Close to ____% of girls in Bangladesh are married by the age of 18.

3. Watermelons are ____% water.

4. In the USA, ____% of employees eat lunch and work at the same time.

5. ____% of American adults go on a diet each year.

6. ____% of divorced women eventually remarry.

7. ____% of dog and cat owners carry pictures of their pets in their wallets.

8. ____% of all food in the world intended for human consumption is lost or wasted.

9. ____% of the world's construction cranes are currently in Dubai.

10. ____% of an iceberg is underwater.

Game No. 28
How long quiz

'Have you been waiting long?'

How to play the game

Teams/individuals.

Preparation: Photocopy the sheet and distribute it among the teams/individuals.

The idea of the game: To get points by answering the questions correctly.

Playing the game: Give each team/individual a few minutes to complete the quiz. Award three points for a correct answer. If no one has the correct answer award one point to the team/individual that is closest. The team/individual with the most points wins the game.

1. How long did it take to clear Ground Zero?   ____ months ____ days

2. How long is the Grand Canyon?   _____ km

3. How long did it take to build
   the Eiffel Tower   ____ years ____ months

4. How long was the first moonwalk?   _____

5. What is the world record for holding
   your breath under water?   _____

6. How long is the Channel Tunnel?   _____ km

7. How long is a marathon
   to the nearest kilometre?   _____ km

8. How long is a round
   in a professional boxing match?   _____ minutes

9. How long is the half-time break
   in a football match?   _____ minutes

10. How long is a fortnight?   _____

Multiple-choice quizzes

How to play the game

Teams/individuals.

Preparation: Photocopy the sheet and distribute it among the teams/individuals.

The idea of the game: To get points by choosing the correct questions.

Playing the game: Each team/individual is given a few minutes to answer the questions. The team/individual with the most correct answers wins the game.

The name game

1. **What are you doing if you are 'bobbing up and down'?**
   a. exercises
   b. drinking
   c. going up and down

2. **If someone is 'taking the mickey', what are they doing?**
   a. making fun of you
   b. praying
   c. stealing

3. **If you 'go to the John', where do you go?**
   a. to school
   b. to work
   c. to the toilet

4. **If you 'jack something in', what do you do?**
   a stop it
   b start it
   c pay for it

5. **What's a 'nancy boy'?**
   a. a hard, macho guy
   b. a softie
   c. a womaniser

6. **Someone who is thin is referred to as:**
   a. slim **Stan**
   b. slim **Steve**
   c. slim **Jim**

7. **What happens if something 'peters out'?**
   a. it loses momentum and slowly stops
   b. it keeps going on forever
   c. it becomes more and more popular

8. **What is a 'Jack of all trades'?**
   a. a lazy person who doesn't work
   b. someone who can do a lot of different jobs well
   c. a womaniser

9. **A 'doubting Thomas' …**
   a. believes you
   b. doesn't believe you
   c. hates you

10. **If you think you are clever, you are …**
    a. a smart **John**
    b. a smart **Susie**
    c. a smart **Alec**

11. **An unattractive woman is known as …**
    a. plain **Jane**
    b. bland **Barbara**
    c. pale **Pauline**

12. **A reliable person is referred to as:**
    a. steady **Teddy**
    b. steady **Freddi**
    c. steady **Eddy**

13. **A nervous woman is called:**
    a. a shrinking **Silvia**
    b. a shrinking **Violet**
    c. a shrinking **Susie**

14. **If you are content, you could be:**
    a. as happy as **Harry**
    b. as happy as **Larry**
    c. as happy as **Henry**

Colloquial English quiz

1. If someone told you they were **'going for a kip'**, would they be going:
   a. to bed
   b. to a supermarket
   c. to a nightclub

2. If someone said they were **'throwing in the towel'**, would they be:
   a. playing a ballgame
   b. giving up
   c. going to bed

3. If someone told you there were **'on edge'**, would they be:
   a. on the phone
   b. very nervous
   c. very relaxed

4. If someone said they were feeling **'under the weather'**, would they be feeling:
   a. sick or tired
   b. full of life and energy
   c. thirsty

5. If someone has **'kicked the bucket'**, does this mean they have:
   a. stopped smoking
   b. died
   c. retired from work

6. If someone told you his colleague was **'a boozer'**, would he mean:
   a. his colleague talked a lot
   b. his colleague was lazy
   c. his colleague drank a lot

7. If someone was **'pulling your leg'**, would they be:
   a. stealing money from you
   b. making fun of you
   c. trying to steal your girlfriend/boyfriend

8. If you were **'chucking up'**, would you be:
   a. being sick
   b. drinking Guinness
   c. playing a board game

9. If something was **'a piece of cake'**, would it be:
   a. very difficult
   b. very stupid
   c. very easy

10. If you described someone as **'a skinflint'**, would they be:
    a. very generous with their money
    b. very mean
    c. a vicar

11. **'The Old Bill'** are:
    a. your parents-in-law
    b. your older brothers
    c. the police

12. If someone is **'up the spout'**, they are:
    a. pregnant
    b. drunk
    c. angry

13. If you were **'doing porridge'**, you'd be:
    a. eating breakfast
    b. in prison
    c. working very hard

Just a job

1. **What would you take to a cobbler?**
   a. a sick pet
   b. your shoes
   c. dirty laundry

2. **What gets cleaned at a dry cleaners?**
   a. clothes
   b. windows
   c. cars

3. **What do you do at a pawnbrokers?**
   a. buy magazines
   b. sell your possessions
   c. play games

4. **What does an undertaker deal with?**
   a. meat
   b. dead bodies
   c. insurance

5. **What does a taxidermist stuff?**
   a. pillows
   b. dead animals
   c. olives

6. **If someone told you he was a copper, would he work:**
   a. in a fire station
   b. in a bus station
   c. in a police station

7. **Does a chippie work with:**
   a. metal
   b. plastic
   c. wood

8. **If you went to a shrink, would you have:**
   a. eating problems
   b. psychological problems
   c. money problems

9. **If you went to the quack, would you be:**
   a. sick
   b. wanting to borrow money
   c. looking for a new car

10. **What is a cowboy?**
    a. a worker who works well
    b. a worker who doesn't do the job properly
    c. the boss of a building site

11. **A seamstress will:**
    a. repair your clothes
    b. prepare a meal for you
    c. fix your car

12. **If you went to a landlord in a pub, what would he do?**
    a. let you in
    b. take your coat
    c. pour you a drink

13. **Where would you find a bouncer?**
    a. on a football pitch
    b. at the door of a nightclub
    c. at the swimming pool

14. **What does a navvie do?**
    a. dig holes
    b. navigate
    c. drive a taxi

15. **What does a joiner do?**
    a. register members in a club
    b. glue things together
    c. make furniture

General knowledge

1. **What is the most common street name in Britain?**
a. High Street
b. London Road
c. West Street

2. **Which British city has more miles of canal than Venice?**
a. London
b. Brighton
c. Birmingham

3. **Who lives at Clarence House?**
a. Prince Philip
b. Prince Charles
c. Prince Edward

4. **What is the most popular sport to feature in films?**
a. football
b. car racing
c. boxing

5. **Which two Beatles were left handed?**
a. Paul & Ringo
b. Paul & John
c. Paul & George

6. **What is the fastest animal on two legs?**
a. chicken
b. ostrich
c. flamingo

7. **It is impossible to cry in space.**
a. true
b. false

8. **Thomas Edison, who invented the light bulb, was afraid of the dark.**
a. true
b. false

9. **What is the most used letter in the English Language?**
a. e
b. t
c. a

10. **Most Eskimos have fridges.**
a. true
b. false

11. **What nationality was Chopin?**
a. Polish
b. German
c. Austrian

12. **What is heavier?**
a. a kilo of sand
b. a kilo of feathers
c. both the same

13. **What's the highest mountain in the world?**
a. Kilimanjaro
b. Fuji
c. Everest

14. **Which foot did Neil Armstrong put on the moon first?**
a. left
b. right
c. both

15. **Where were the first Olympic Games held?**
a. Rome
b. Athens
c. Baden-Baden

Certified success

1. **New-born babies need:**
   a. a birth certificate
   b. a born certificate
   c. a baby birth certificate

2. **A doctor must sign this if someone dies:**
   a. a dead certificate
   b. a death certificate
   c. a stiff as a board certificate

3. **A driving licence is issued by the DVLA, which stands for:**
   a. Driver and Vehicle Licensing Agency
   b. Driver and Vehicle Leasing Agency
   c. Drunks and Vandals Lunatic Agency

4. **The English equivalent of the 'Abitur' is:**
   a. abuture
   b. 'A' Levels
   c. degree

5. **All adults in England must carry an identity card at all times.**
   a. true
   b. false

6. **Policemen in Britain can issue 'on the spot' fines.**
   a. true
   b. false

7. **Immigrants seeking British citizenship must pass a test to prove they know about British life, history and culture.**
   a. true
   b. false

8. **Voting in England is compulsory**
   a. true
   b. false

9. **If you are sick, your doctor needs to give you:**
   a. a sick certificate
   b. a certificate of sickness
   c. a sick note

10. **C of E means:**
    a. Certificate of Education
    b. Church of England

11. **'A dead cert' is:**
    a. a certificate which is no longer valid
    b. an absolute certainty

12. **TÜV in English is:**
    a. MOT certificate
    b. road worthy certificate
    c. automobile certificate

13. **'Gewerbeschein' in English is:**
    a. trade certificate
    b. trading certificate
    c. business certificate

14. **If you go bananas, you are 'certified insane':**
    a. true
    b. false

Game No. 30
German/English vocabulary quizzes

'I'm a policeman. We are also known as the fuzz, the cops, the peelers, the pigs, the rozzers, the scum, the filth, and the boys in blue.'

How to play the game

Teams/individuals.

Preparation: Photocopy the sheet and distribute it among the teams/individuals.

The idea of the game: To get points by choosing the correct questions.

Playing the game: Each team/individual is given a few minutes to answer the questions. The team/individual with the most correct answers wins the game.

Choose the correct English word

1. Notausgang ☒

- emergency way ☐
- emergency out ☐
- emergency way out ☐
- emergency exit ☐

2. Mutterschaftsurlaub ☒

- baby break ☐
- mother time ☐
- maternity leave ☐
- parent leave ☐

3. Mädchenname ☒

- girl name ☐
- before name ☐
- maiden name ☐
- single name ☐

4. Hochzeitstag ☒

- wedding remembrance day ☐
- marriage day ☐
- wedding anniversary ☐
- marriage remember day ☐

5. Mehrwertsteuer ☒

- more value tax ☐
- value added tax ☐
- selling tax ☐
- value tax ☐

6. Kindergeld ☒

- child's money ☐
- children money ☐
- family money ☐
- family allowance ☐

7. Aufenthaltserlaubnis ☒

- stay visa ☐
- visitor visa ☐
- foreign national visa ☐
- residence permit ☐

8. Kaiserschnitt ☒

- emperor cut ☐
- caesarean section ☐
- stomach delivery ☐
- emergency delivery cut ☐

9. Doppelgänger ☒

- same ☐
- double goer ☐
- double ☐
- twin looker ☐

10. Fangfrage ☒

- capture question ☐
- catch out question ☐
- trick question ☐
- clutch question ☐

Choose the correct English word

1. Teufelskreis ☒
- devil's circle ☐
- dread circle ☐
- devil's ring ☐
- vicious circle ☐

2. Brückentag ☒
- bridge day ☐
- gap day ☐
- extra holiday day ☐
- bridging up day ☐

3. Ausbildung ☒
- train ☐
- trainer time ☐
- apprenticeship ☐
- educationing ☐

4. vor Ort ☒
- situation ☐
- at location ☐
- at site ☐
- on site ☐

5. Blockflöte ☒
- block flute ☐
- black flute ☐
- recorder ☐
- recorder flute ☐

6. Einwegflasche ☒
- one-way bottle ☐
- once bottle ☐
- disposable bottle ☐
- bring bottle ☐

7. Pfand ☒
- deposit ☐
- secure payment ☐
- return payment ☐
- pan payment ☐

8. Kontoüberziehung ☒
- overflow ☐
- overdraft ☐
- overgone ☐
- overgo ☐

9. Girokonto ☒
- current account ☐
- actual account ☐
- day to day account ☐
- giro account ☐

10. Baugenehmigung ☒
- plan allowance ☐
- building allowance ☐
- planning permission ☐
- building permission ☐

Choose the correct English word

1. Kopfsalat ☒
head salad	☐
head lettuce	☐
lettuce	☐
salad	☐

2. Kopf hoch! ☒
head off	☐
chin up	☐
head high	☐
chin high	☐

3. Kopf an Kopf ☒
head on head	☐
head for head	☐
neck and neck	☐
neck to head	☐

4. Kopf runter! ☒
duck!	☐
chicken!	☐
pig!	☐
penguin!	☐

5. aus dem Kopf ☒
by heart	☐
by head	☐
by brain	☐
by bye!	☐

6. Kopf oder Zahl? ☒
heads or numbers?	☐
heads or amounts?	☐
heads or tails?	☐
head or?	☐

7. Kopfschmerzen ☒
headpain	☐
headache	☐
headscare	☐
headie	☐

8. auf dem Kopf stehen ☒
to stay on your head	☐
to stand on your head	☐
to be head over up	☐
heads up	☐

9. mit dem Kopf stoßen ☒
to nut	☐
to peanut	☐
to Brazil nut	☐
to nutty	☐

10. Kopfball ☒
head ball	☐
heads ball	☐
header	☐
heading ball	☐

Choose the correct English word

1. Buggy	☒
pushchair	☐
baby wagon	☐
child's wagon	☐
children wagon	☐

6. Perücke	☒
perrucke	☐
hair spare	☐
wig	☐
hair wig	☐

2. Zylinder	☒
cylinder	☐
big hat	☐
flat hat	☐
tophat	☐

7. Bauchnabel	☒
stomach button	☐
belly button	☐
stomach hole	☐
belly hole	☐

3. Nichtraucher	☒
no smoker	☐
not smoker	☐
non-smoker	☐
no smoking	☐

8. Kreuzfahrt	☒
cross journey	☐
ship ferry	☐
cruise	☐
liner journey	☐

4. Silvester	☒
Silvester	☐
New Year's Day	☐
New Year's Eve	☐
Newly year	☐

9. Quittung	☒
payment proof	☐
recipe	☐
bill	☐
receipt	☐

5. unvorhergesehen	☒
non-seeable	☐
not seeable	☐
unforeseen	☐
not future seen	☐

10. Achterbahn	☒
railroad ride	☐
rollercoaster	☐
eight drive ride	☐
dipper	☐

Choose the correct English word

1. leblos ☒
- inanimate ☐
- unanimate ☐
- imanimate ☐
- animate ☐

2. reparieren ☒
- (to) overhaul ☐
- (to) overall ☐
- (to) overhall ☐
- (to) oberall ☐

3. Dachboden ☒
- ottic ☐
- attich ☐
- attic ☐
- attack ☐

4. spotten ☒
- (to) cheer ☐
- (to) sneer ☐
- (to) peer ☐
- (to) jeer ☐

5. staunen ☒
- (to) ape ☐
- (to) nape ☐
- (to) gape ☐
- (to) wape ☐

6. verhindern ☒
- (to) thwart ☐
- (to) tart ☐
- (to) twart ☐
- (to) twirt ☐

7. Arbeitskittel ☒
- a smack ☐
- a smeck ☐
- a speck ☐
- a smock ☐

8. Trödelmarkt ☒
- mumble sale ☐
- tumble sale ☐
- jumble sale ☐
- rumble sale ☐

9. rütteln ☒
- (to) jolt ☐
- (to) rolt ☐
- (to) bolt ☐
- (to) salt ☐

10. Weisheitszahn ☒
- wise tooth ☐
- sage tooth ☐
- wisdom tooth ☐
- wiseman's tooth ☐

Answers

Game No. 2 – Bizarre world records (1)

1. Typing to one million: **16 years, seven months**
2. World's largest house of cards: **219,000**
3. Most t-shirts worn at one time: **121**
4. World's largest rubber band ball: **175,000 rubber bands**
5. World's oldest prostitute: **82 years**
6. World's oldest father: **90 years**
7. World's largest naked photo shoot: **18,000**
8. Highest bungee jump: **233 metres**

Game No. 2 – Bizarre world records (2)

1. Fastest time to duct tape a person to the wall: **96 seconds**
2. Most t-shirts folded in one minute: **23**
3. World's longest handshake: **12 hours, 34 seconds**
4. Most spoons balanced on the face: **17**
5. Biggest English breakfast eaten: **2.9 kilos**
6. Most people in a smart car: **16**
7. Fastest time to dress a Barbie doll: **30 seconds**
8. Longest bridal veil: **3.36 km**

Game No. 2 – Bizarre world records (3)

1. Sitting in a bath of ice: **72 minutes**
2. Lifting weights with an ear: **61 kilos**
3. Most straws in the mouth: **264**
4. Most cosmetic surgery operations: **47**
5. Most times married: **23**
6. Simultaneous kissing: **39,898 people**
7. Most people dressed as Santa Claus: **12,965**
8. Most litres of beer glasses carried by a woman: **19**

Game No. 2 – Bizarre world records (4)

1. World's biggest barbecue: **1250** people brought food and cooked
2. World's longest bridge: **32.5 km**
3. World record number of body piercings: **4250**
4. Juggling: Most balls kept in the air at the same time: **11**

5. Heaviest car balanced on the head: **159 kilos**
6. Highest stiletto: **40 cm**
7. World's oldest person: **122 years**
8. World's biggest cupcake: **68 kilos**

Game No. 2 – Bizarre world records (5)

1. Running 100 metres on ice: **17.35 seconds**
2. Fastest time to eat a 12' pizza: **105 seconds**
3. Most cockroaches eaten in one minute: **36**
4. Heaviest aircraft pulled by one man: **187 tons**
5. Most press-ups using the back of the hands in one hour: **1,940**
6. World's longest cigar: **81.8 metres**
7. World's biggest omelette: **110,000 eggs**
8. World's biggest onion: **8 kilos**

Game No. 3 – Numbers quiz (1)

1. How many days in April, May and June? **91**
2. How many different values of British coins are in circulation? **8**
3. Which A do you get if you halve a sheet of A4 paper? **A5**
4. What's 20% of 2000? **400**
5. How many bits in a byte? **8**
6. How many symphonies did Beethoven write? **9**
7. How many legs on an ant? **6**
8. How many sides on a 50 pence piece? **7**
9. How many stripes on the Stars & Stripes? **13**
10. Queen Victoria reigned for how many years? **63**
11. What is the gestation period in days of the African elephant? **660**
12. How many mm in a km? **1 million**
13. How many capsules on the London Eye? **32**
14. In what year was Walt Disney's Jungle Book film released? **1967**
15. How many players on the court in a basketball team? **5**

Game No. 3 – Numbers quiz (2)

1. How many lives does a cat have? **9**
2. How many dominoes in a normal set? **28**
3. How many wheels on a unicycle? **1**
4. What's the maximum number of golf clubs you can use in a tournament? **14**
5. If you are happy you are on cloud what? **9**
6. How many inches in a yard? **36**
7. How many seasons in Vivaldi's composition? **4**
8. How many tails on a Manx cat? **0**
9. How many eyes on a cyclops? **1**
10. To the nearest kilometre, how long is the Channel Tunnel? **50**
11. How old was the oldest man in space? **77**

12. How many spikes on the Statue of Liberty's head? **7**
13. How many wheels on a tandem? **2**
14. How many plays did Shakespeare write? **39**
15. Around the world in how many days? **80**

Game No. 3 – Numbers quiz (3)

1. What does the Roman number L stand for? **50**
2. How many questions must you answer correctly to win one million on 'Who Wants To Be A Millionaire'? **15**
3. What's the maximum number you can score with three darts? **180**
4. Unlucky ... **13**
5. How many Nobel prizes are presented each year? **6**
6. If you are blissfully happy, you are in **seventh** heaven.
7. How many seconds in an hour? **3600**
8. How many hours in a week? **168**
9. How many black keys on a standard piano? **36**
10. How many colours in a rainbow? **7**
11. How many reindeer does Santa's sleigh have? **9** (Rudolph, Dasher, Dancer, Prancer, Vixen, Donder, Blitzen, Cupid and Comet.)
12. How many strings on a 12-string guitar? **12, of course!**
13. The lowest temperature ever recorded on earth was minus what? **−89° C** (At the Soviet Vostok Station in Antarctica, on July 21, 1983.)
14. What is the highest temperature recorded on Earth? **57° C** (Recorded in Death Valley on July 10, 1913.)
15. What is Russia's population to the nearest million? **143 million**

Game No. 4 – Odd man out (1)

1. Otto / Mum / **Tom** / Dad
   (All the other words are palindromes – they spell the same backwards.)
2. **Man** / Assessment / City / Call
   (All the other words go with the word 'centre'.)
3. Match / Game / **Play** / Set
   (Tennis – 'Game, set & match.')
4. Die / Fall / Boot / **New**
   (All the other words could also be German words.)
5. **Talk** / Speak / Tell / Write
   (All the other verbs are irregular.)
6. Happy / Grumpy / **Moody** / Sleepy
   (Moody is not one of the seven dwarfs.)
7. King / Queen / **Prince** / Supertramp
   (All the others are groups, Prince is a solo artist.)
8. **2010** / 1804 / 2400 / 2000
   (2010 is not a leap year, the rest are.)
9. George Michael / Rod Stewart / Cliff Richard / **Tom Jones**
   (All the other singers' names are made up of first names.)

10. Nürnberg	**Berlin**	Frankfurt	Thüringen

(All the others are also sausages.)

11. **Knife**	Junction	Time	Bone

(All the others go with t.)

12. Street	James	Personal	**Call**

(All the others go with Bond.)

13. **Golf**	Handball	Football	Basketball

(All the others are team sports.)

14. York	Delhi	Hampshire	**Boston**

(All the others go with 'new'.)

15. Chester	Made	Kind	**Woman**

(All the others go with 'man'.)

Game No. 4 – Odd man out (2)

1. **River**	Arms	Cot	Pram

(All the others hold babies.)

2. **Carol**	Anita	Anna	Bob

(All the other names start and end with the same letter.)

3. **Ronald Reagan**	John F. Kennedy	Martin Luther King	Yitzhak Rabin

(All were shot, only Reagan survived.)

4. Snow	Ice Cubes	Ice Cream	**Cocoa**

(All the others melt.)

5. Umbrellas	**Rain**	Petrol Prices	Taxes

(All the others go up, rain comes down.)

6. **Brazil**	Argentina	America	Australia

(All the others start and end with A.)

6. Andrew	Edward	Anne	**George**

(All the others are Queen Elizabeth II's children.)

8. Abba	The Corrs	**Queen**	Blondie

(Queen, all the others have female singers.)

9. Sweden	Denmark	Uk	**Germany**

(All the others do not yet have the euro.)

10. **Die Toten Hosen**	Gildo Horn	Lena	Stefan Raab

(All the others have represented Germany in the Eurovision Song Contest.)

11. **Spider**	Ant	Beetle	Bee

(A spider has eight legs, all the others have six.)

12. Heaven 17	Boyz 11 Men	4 Non Blondes	**Men At Work**

(All the others have numbers in their names.)

13. Bahamas	Jamaica	Indonesia	**Thailand**

(All the others are island countries.)

14. **Roy**	Charlie	Lesley	Stevie

(All the others could be boys or girls.)

15. Italy	**Spanish**	France	Germany

(Spanish is a nationality, all the others are countries.)

Game No. 5 – True or false? (1)

1. Camels are born without humps. — **TRUE**
2. Mel Gibson was one of 10 children. — **FALSE – 11**
3. Sharks are immune to all known diseases. — **TRUE**
4. 1000 quarter-pound hamburgers can be made out of one cow. — **FALSE – only 400**
5. 'Dr Jekyll and Mr Hyde' is the most filmed story of all time. — **FALSE – Dracula**
6. Cats are the most popular pet in America. — **TRUE – 66 million (dogs 58 million)**
7. Only male mosquitoes bite. — **FALSE – female**
8. The only thing that can destroy a diamond is intense heat. — **TRUE**
9. An octopus has two hearts. — **FALSE – three**
10. Beethoven had a photographic memory. — **FALSE – Mozart**
11. Krakow has a Pope John Paul II airport. — **TRUE**
12. Boxer George Foreman named all his four sons George. — **TRUE**
13. Lettuce is 85% water. — **FALSE – 97%**
14. Beef is the most popular kind of meat in the world. — **FALSE – pork**
15. Walt Disney was afraid of mice. — **TRUE**

All or Nothing Last Question:
The loudest animal in the world is the African elephant. — **FALSE – Blue whale (188 decibels)**

Game No. 5 – True or false? (2)

1. The first Englishman to be killed in a plane crash was Charles Rolls of Rolls-Royce fame. — **TRUE**
2. Blues legend Muddy Waters was the first recording artist to receive a gold disc. — **FALSE – Glenn Miller**
3. The first supermarket in the world was in America. — **FALSE – France**
4. The world's first cash machine was in London, England. — **TRUE**
5. A hippo is born under water. — **TRUE**
6. Vincent Van Gogh only sold one painting while he was alive. — **TRUE – The Red Vineyard**
7. No word in the English language rhymes with pint. — **TRUE**
8. The hummingbird is the only bird that can fly backwards. — **TRUE**
9. There was once a town in West Virginia called '9'. — **FALSE – it was called '6'**
10. The average person spends two months of their lifetime waiting for traffic lights to change. — **FALSE – two weeks**
11. The most visited country in the world is the USA. — **FALSE – France**
12. There is a George Bush airport in Houston. — **TRUE**
13. 13 people have walked on the moon. — **FALSE – 12**

14. Winston Churchill had a stammer when he was a young boy. **TRUE**
15. Bill Clinton & Bill Gates have photographic memories. **TRUE**

All or Nothing Last Question:
The last song Elvis sang in public was 'My Way'. **FALSE – Bridge over troubled Water**

Game No. 5 – True or false? (3)

1. Our nose, eyes and ears never stop growing until the day we die. **FALSE**
2. The most common first name in the world is Mohammed. **TRUE**
3. No word in the English language has five consecutive letters that are vowels. **FALSE – queueing**
4. If a month starts on a Sunday it will contain Friday the 13th. **TRUE**
5. There are only 25 countries world-wide in which people drive on the left hand side of the road. **FALSE – about 50**
6. The youngest ever Pope was only 12 years old. **FALSE – 11**
7. Diamond is the hardest natural substance on earth. **TRUE**
8. More than 1.5 million people die each year from malaria. **TRUE**
9. More than a third of adults hit the snooze button at least three times before they get up. **TRUE**
10. In the English version of the game 'Monopoly', Old Kent Road is the most valuable property. **FALSE – the cheapest**
11. Bagpipes were invented not by the Scottish, but by the Romans. **TRUE**
12. 'Happy Birthday' was the first song to be performed in outer space, sung by the Apollo IX astronauts on March 8, 1969. **TRUE**
13. Jimi Hendrix, Janis Joplin, and Jim Morrison were all 26 years old when they died. **FALSE – 27**
14. The 1st feature-length animated film released by Disney Studios was 'The Jungle Book'. **FALSE – 'Snow White'**
15. Jim Morrison (of the 60's rock group The Doors) was the first rock star to be arrested on stage. **TRUE**

All or Nothing Last Question:
China's Beijing Duck Restaurant can seat 8,000 people at one time. **FALSE – 9,000!**

Game No. 5 – True or false? (4)

1. Australia is the only country that is also a continent. **TRUE**
2. According to German researchers, the risk of heart attack is higher on Sunday than any other day of the week. **FALSE – Monday**

3. It takes 17 muscles to frown – 43 to smile. **FALSE – the other way round**

4. A zebra is black with white stripes. **FALSE**

5. German Shepherds bite humans more than any other breed of dog. **TRUE**

6. Large kangaroos cover more than 10 metres with each jump. **TRUE**

7. No word in the English language rhymes with orange. **TRUE**

8. 'Rhythms' is the longest English word without a vowel. **TRUE**

9. The shortest war on record, between Britain and Zanzibar in 1896, lasted just 38 hours. **FALSE – 38 minutes**

10. There are over 200 rooms in the White House. **FALSE – 132**

11. Cashews are the only nuts mentioned in the Bible. **FALSE – Pistachios**

12. When Coca Cola was first produced it was green. **TRUE**

13. The lead singer of the band Toto shot and killed himself in a game of Russian Roulette in 1978. His last words were, 'Don't worry, it's not loaded.' **FALSE – lead singer of the band Chicago**

14. The parachute was invented by Leonardo da Vinci. **TRUE**

15. Disney World is bigger than the world's 15 smallest countries. **FALSE – 5**

All or Nothing Last Question:
Two out of every ten people who come to a party in your home will look in your bathroom cabinet. **FALSE – four out of ten!!**

Game No. 5 – True or false? (5)

1. There was once a Society for the Prevention of People Being Buried Alive. **TRUE**

2. You share your birthday with at least 90 million others. **FALSE – 9 million**

3. Only seven men have ever known the formula for Coca-Cola. **TRUE**

4. The Greek national anthem has 148 verses. **FALSE – 158**

5. Beethoven was once arrested for being a tramp. **TRUE**

6. When the Star Wars director George Lucas said the legendary words 'May the force be with you' at a press conference, an interpreter for the German TV channel N24 translated the words as 'Am 4. Mai sind wir bei Ihnen.' **TRUE**

7. According to an old law, women in Memphis, Tennessee were only allowed to drive if a man walked in front of the car waving a red flag as a warning sign to other drivers. **TRUE**

8. An average woman spends 16 days of her life rummaging in her handbag. **FALSE – 76 days**

9. Franz Beckenbauer has already appeared in advertisements for five different makes of car. **FALSE – six**

10. Half of the dog owners in Germany buy
    Christmas presents for their dogs.   **FALSE – two thirds**
11. In Newfoundland, Canada there is a place
    called 'Vibrator'   **FALSE – it's called 'Dildo'**
12. In the German telephone directories there are
    around 1.2 million different surnames.   **TRUE**
13. Prince William's nickname when he was at
    St Andrews University was 'Big Willy'.   **False – 'P Willy'**
14. A 1997 survey found that about 90% of
    American workers would like to fire their boss.   **TRUE**
15. 47% of all statistics are made up.   **TRUE**

All or Nothing Last Question:
Elvis Presley never toured outside the United States.   **TRUE**

Game No. 6 – Double trouble quiz

1. **90%** of all newly-opened restaurants fail in the first year. Of the ones that survive, **90%** fail in the second year.
2. King Mongut of Siam had **9,000** wives, but was quoted as saying he only loved **700** of them.
3. In the 1950s **80%** of chickens in Europe were free-range. By 1980 it was only **1%**.
4. **15 million** blood cells are produced and destroyed in the human body **every second**.
5. Every year **100** people choke to death on **biros**.
6. In Kentucky **50%** of people getting married for the first time are under **20** years of age.
7. Americans eat approximately **20** billion **pickles** every year.
8. **David** is the most common name in **the Bible**.
9. **Worker** bees are all **female**.
10. **82%** of the workers building the Panama Canal – which opened in 1914 – suffered from **malaria**.
11. In Africa more people are killed by **crocodiles** than by **lions**.
12. Julio Iglesias once had five gallons of water flown from Miami to **LA** so he could wash his **hair**.
13. **Potatoes** are the biggest-selling frozen vegetable in **the world**.
14. **The Sun** is 300,300 times bigger than **the Earth**.
15. There are **20,000** thousand living organisms in a glass of **water**.
16. The average **koala bear** sleeps **22 hours** a day.
17. A typical American eats **28** pigs in **a lifetime**.
18. 4,000 years ago in **Egypt**, the penalty for killing a cat was **death**.
19. When left alone with a tea cosy, **98%** of **men** will put it on their heads.
20. During the **Second** World War, the American automobile industry produced **139** cars.

Game No. 7 – Words quiz (1) – Beautiful words

1. mother — **Mutter**
2. passion — **Leidenschaft**
3. (to) smile — **lächeln**
4. eternity — **Ewigkeit**
5. destiny — **Schicksal**
6. lullaby — **Wiegenlied**
7. liberty — **Freiheit**
8. peace — **Frieden**
9. tranquility — **Ruhe**
10. sweetheart — **Schatz**
11. hope — **Hoffnung**
12. rainbow — **Regenbogen**
13. (to) tickle — **kitzeln**
14. paradox — **Paradox**
15. sophisticated — **anspruchsvoll**
16. cute — **niedlich**
17. cosy — **gemütlich**
18. hilarious — **urkomisch**
19. lollipop — **Lutscher**
20. bumblebee — **Hummel**
21. flabbergasted — **baff**
22. hiccup — **Schluckauf**
23. hen night — **Junggesellinnenabschied**
24. hippopotamus — **Nilpferd**
25. whoops — **hoppla**
26. butterfly — **Schmetterling**
27. peek-a-boo — **Guck-guck-Spiel**
28. shipshape — **tipptopp**
29. gorgeous — **wunderschön**
30. bubble — **Blase**

Game No. 7 – Words quiz (2) – Young and old vocabulary

1. pension — **Rente**
2. milk teeth — **Milchzähne**
3. healthy — **gesund**
4. grandparents — **Großeltern**
5. grandchildren — **Enkelkinder**
6. zimmer frame — **Rollator**
7. dummy — **Schnuller**
8. pocket money — **Taschengeld**
9. false teeth — **dritte Zähne**
10. bib — **Schlabberlätzchen**
11. slide — **Rutsche**

12. old-age pension	**Altersrente**
13. care home	**Pflegeheim**
14. playground	**Spielplatz**
15. exams	**Prüfungen**
16. meals on wheels	**Essen auf Rädern**
17. social worker	**Sozialarbeiter**
18. midwife	**Hebamme**
19. swing	**Schaukel**
20. old folks' home	**Altenheim**
21. retirement	**Ruhestand**
22. potty training	**Töpfchentraining**
23. spot	**Pickel**
24. first kiss	**erster Kuss**
25. school report	**Schulzeugnis**
26. wedding anniversary	**Hochzeitstag**
27. retirement home	**Altenheim**
28. spry	**agil**
29. sweets	**Süßigkeiten**
30. cry-baby	**Heulsuse**

Game No. 7 – Words quiz (3) – Pub vocabulary

1. a pub crawl	**eine Kneipentour**
2. 'It's your round!'	**,Deine Runde!'**
3. drayman	**Bierkutscher**
4. 'Last orders!'	**'Letzte Runde!'**
5. draught beer	**Fassbier**
6. bottled beer	**Flaschenbier**
7. pork scratchings	**Speckchips**
8. crisps	**Kartoffelchips**
9. pool	**Poolbilliard**
10. darts	**Dart**
11. spirits	**Spirituosen**
12. beer mat	**Bierdeckel**
13. landlord	**Wirt**
14. ashtray	**Aschenbecher**
15. barmaid	**Kellnerin**
16. a pint	**ein Pint**
17. a dive	**eine Spelunke**
18. barrels	**Fässer**
19. cellar	**Keller**
20. country pub	**Dorfkneipe**
21. brewery	**Brauerei**
22. hand pump	**Handpumpe**
23. hops	**Hopfen**

24. pay at the bar	**an der Theke zahlen**
25. pub grub	**Kneipenessen**
26. hangover	**Kater**
27. bartender	**Kellner**
28. underage drinking	**Alkoholkonsum bei Minderjährigen**
29. happy hour	**Happy Hour**
30. binge drinking	**Kampftrinken**

Game No. 7 – Words quiz (4) – Shopping vocabulary

1. shopping trolley	**Einkaufswagen**
2. the till	**die Kasse**
3. receipt	**Quittung**
4. shoplifter	**Ladendieb**
5. poultry	**Geflügel**
6. scales	**Waage**
7. check out	**die Kasse**
8. shop assistant	**Verkäufer/in**
9. store detective	**Kaufhausdetektiv**
10. in stock	**auf Lager**
11. out of stock	**nicht vorrätig**
12. down payment	**Anzahlung**
13. instalments	**Raten**
14. interest free credit	**zinsloser Kredit**
15. special offer	**Sonderangebot**
16. sale	**Schlussverkauf**
17. closing down sale	**Ausverkauf**
18. clearance sale	**Räumungsverkauf**
19. barcode	**Barcode**
20. newsagent	**Zeitungsladen**
21. off license	**Getränkemarkt**
22. discount	**Rabatt**
23. VAT	**Mehrwertsteuer**
24. deposit	**Anzahlung/Kaution**
25. shelves	**Regale**
26. aisles	**Gänge**
27. shopping basket	**Einkaufs-/Warenkorb**
28. small change	**Kleingeld**
29. short-changed	**(um sein Wechselgeld) geprellt**
30. reduced	**reduziert**

Game No. 7 – Words quiz (5) – Holiday vocabulary

1. currency	**Währung**
2. long-haul flight	**Langstreckenflug**
3. domestic flight	**Inlandsflug**

4.	a leg of a journey	**Etappe**
5.	(to be) frisked	**gefilzt werden**
6.	B&B	**Übernachtung mit Frühstück**
7.	half board	**Halbpension**
8.	full board	**Vollpension**
9.	self catering	**Selbstversorgung**
10.	abroad	**im Ausland**
11.	turbulence	**Turbulenzen**
12.	suntan	**Sonnenbräune**
13.	phrasebook	**Sprachführer**
14.	off the beaten track	**abseits ausgetretener Pfade**
15.	(to) get ripped off	**abgezockt werden**
16.	package holiday	**Pauschalreise**
17.	off-peak	**außerhalb der Hauptsaison**
18.	flight	**Flug**
19.	duty free	**zollfrei**
20.	customs	**Zoll**
21.	local cuisine	**Regionalküche**
22.	local knowledge	**Ortskenntnis**
23.	guided tour	**Führung**
24.	pickpocket	**Tachendieb**
25.	tourist attraction	**Sehenswürdigkeit**
26.	chambermaid	**Zimmermädchen**
27.	pool bar	**Poolbar**
28.	the old town	**die Altstadt**
29.	holiday romance	**Urlaubsromanze**
30.	tour operator	**Reiseveranstalter**

Game No. 10 – Name the day (1)

	Event	*Date*
1.	Neil Armstrong walked on the moon	20th July, 1969
2.	Soviet Union's Yuri Gagarin became the first man in space	12th April, 1961
3.	The U. S. dropped the atomic bomb on Hiroshima	3rd September, 1945
4.	Germany invaded Poland	1st September, 1939
5.	Live Aid	13th July, 1985
6.	Assassination of JFK	22nd November, 1963
7.	England won the World Cup at Wembley	30th July, 1966
8.	Building began on the Berlin Wall	13th August, 1961
9.	The Berlin Wall came down	9th November, 1989
10.	The Beatles split	10th April, 1970

Game No. 10 – Name the day quiz (2)

Event	Date
1. Attack on the Twin Towers in New York	11th September, 2001
2. The assassination of Martin Luther King	4th April, 1968
3. The sinking of the Titanic	14th April, 1912
4. Nelson Mandela freed from prison in South Africa	11th February, 1990
5. Prince Charles and Princess Diana marry at Westminster Abbey	29th July, 1981
6. The First World War ends	11th November, 1918
7. Princess Diana dies in a car crash in Paris	31st August, 1997
8. Concorde crashes on take-off in Paris	25th July, 2000
9. Germany last won the World Cup	8th July, 1990
10. Angela Merkel becomes Chancellor of Germany	18th September, 2005

Game No. 12 – How old were they? (1)

Name	Age
1. Juliet	13
2. John Lennon	40
3. JFK	46
4. Marilyn Monroe	36
5. Winston Churchill	90
6. Freddie Mercury	45
7. Michael Jackson	50
8. John Wayne	72
9. Karl Marx	65
10. Osama Bin Laden	54

Game No. 12 – How old were they? (2)

Name	Age
1. Jimi Hendrix	27
2. Amy Winehouse	27
3. Janis Joplin	27
4. Jim Morrison	27
5. Kurt Cobain	27
6. The Queen Mother	101
7. James Dean	24
8. Elvis Presley	42
9. Frank Sinatra	82
10. Princess Diana	36

Game No. 13 – Lateral thinking (1)

Poser No. 1 – Solution

Because Sue and Sam were goldfish.

Poser No. 2 – Solution
Use the first two cuts to cut an 'X' in the top of the cake. Now you have four pieces.

Make the third cut horizontal, which will divide the four pieces into eight.

Poser No. 3 – Solution
J
March, **A**pril, **M**ay, **J**une

Poser No. 5 – Solution
Because the last person who took an egg also took the basket with the egg still in it.

Poser No. 4 – Solution
A – keys on a piano

Game No. 13 – Lateral thinking (2)

Poser No. 1 – Solution
He makes **four** trips.
1. He takes the chicken across.
2. He comes back and takes the corn across and comes back with the chicken.
3. He then takes the fox across.
4. He comes back for the chicken.

Poser No. 2 – Solution

S

Donnerstag, **F**reitag, **S**amstag, **S**onntag
German days of the week

Poser No. 3 – Solution

E

Strings on a guitar

Poser No. 4 – Solution

Push the cork into the bottle
and shake the coin out.

Poser No. 5 – Solution

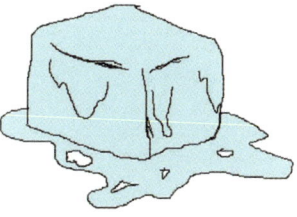

Because they all have telephones!

Game No. 13 – Lateral thinking (3)

Poser No. 1 – Solution

Because the man is a dwarf (he
can't reach the higher buttons).

Poser No. 2 – Solution

He stood on a block of ice (and waited
for it to melt) to hang himself.

Poser No. 3 – Solution

She is a photographer. She shot a
picture of her husband, developed
it, and hung it up to dry.

Poser No. 4 – Solution

yesterday	today	tomorrow
22	23	24

Yesterday, today, and tomorrow!

Poser No. 5 – Solution

The third room. Lions that hadn't eaten
in three years would be dead!

Game No. 14 – Name the other half

Easy (one point)	Medium (two points)	Difficult (three points)
Romeo & Juliet	Abbott & Costello	Alabama Slammer
Laurel & Hardy	Anthony & Cleopatra	Bread & butter
Adam & Eve	Lake District	Act Naturally
Napoleon & Josephine	Get back	Great Yarmouth
Bonnie & Clyde	Land's End	Lovely Rita
Sherlock Holmes & Dr Watson	Nowhere Man	Snowball
Heavy metal	Manhattan	Atlantic Crossing
Dr Jekyll & Mr Hyde	Nowhere Man	New Forest
Simon & Garfunkel	Newcastle	Midlands
Acid house	Monte Carlo	Fame & fortune
Bloody Mary	Thrash metal	Easy Listening
Bucks Fizz	Ragtime	Corpse Reviver
Eleanor Rigby	Torvill & Dean	Dirt cheap
Paperback Writer	Wallace & Gromit	Bonehead
Manchester	Wait & see	Bangers & mash
Great Gatsby	Catch 22	Chalk & cheese
New Delhi	Black Widow	Rockabilly
Cornwall	The Black Death	Mills & Boon
Stonehenge	Big bang	Deathwatch
Hip Hop	Half Man Half Biscuit	Uriah Heep
Free jazz	Kama Sutra	Bubble & Squeak

Game No. 16 – Firsts quiz

1. Wrigley's chewing gum.
2. First American woman in space.
3. Paul Tibbets was the pilot who dropped the first atomic bomb.
4. 'Mr. Watson, come here, I want to see you.' were the first words spoken on the telephone.
5. 'Wait a minute, wait a minute, you ain't heard nothin' yet!' were the first words spoken in a 'talkie' – a film with sound.
6. Richard Nixon was the first US president to resign from office.

Game No. 17 – Who is it?

1. Barrack Obama
2. Robbie Williams
3. Angela Merkel
4. Yoko Ono
5. Vincent Van Gogh
6. James Bond
7. Bill Gates
8. Jesus
9. JR Ewing
10. Christopher Columbus

Game No. 19 – Crazy headlines game

1. Police raid gun shops and find **weapons**
2. Ugliest woman in the world dies after **looking in the mirror**
3. World war two bomber found **on the moon**
4. Double decker bus found **at the North Pole**
5. Fire destroys **crematorium**
6. Sensation! Elvis found alive and well and working in **a fish and chip shop**!
7. Miracle cure **kills** fifth patient!
8. Abraham Lincoln was a **woman**
9. Polishman lost inside LA airport for **18 days**
10. Most earthquake damage caused by **shaking**

Game No. 20 – Quotes of the rich and famous (1)

1. Mae West – 'Be good. And if you can't be good, **be careful**.'
2. Oscar Wilde – 'Life is too short to **learn German**.'
3. John Lennon – 'We are more popular than **Jesus**.'
4. George Best – 'I spent 90% of my money on women, champagne and fast cars. The rest I just **wasted**.'
5. Ivana Trump – 'Girls, don't get mad – get **even**.'

Game No. 20 – Quotes of the rich and famous (2)

1. Winston Churchill – 'You can always count on the Americans to do the right thing. **When they've tried everything else first**.'
2. Groucho Marx – 'I never forget a face, but in your case I will **make an exception**.'
3. George W. Bush – 'I owe a lot to my parents, especially **my mom and dad**.'
4. Radio One DJ – 'And how long have you had this **life-long ambition**?'
5. Gerald Ford – 'Whenever I can, I always watch the Detroit Tigers **on the radio**.'

Game No. 21 – Find the connection game (1)

1. saber-toothed tiger   mammoth   dinosaur
   (All extinct.)
2. die   boot   tag
   (Could all be German words, too.)
3. Simply Red   Pink Floyd   Black Sabbath
   (All have colours in their names.)
4. Paul McCartney   Jimmy Hendrix   Napoleon
   (All left-handed.)
5. George Lazenby   Pierce Brosnan   Roger Moore
   (All played James Bond.)
6. John Lennon   John F. Kennedy   Ronald Reagan
   (All were shot.)
7. moon   velvet   berry hill
   (All go with the word 'blue'.)
8. civic   deed   madam
   (All palindromes – can be spelt backwards.)
9. now   night   not
   (You can put a k in front of each word and make another word.)
10. read   write   wait
    (All sound like another word – read – reed, write – right, wait – weight.)
11. I Don't Want To Talk   Careless Whisper   Shout (Tears for Fears)
    About It (Rod Steward)   (George Michael)
    (All things done with the mouth.)
12. drink   eat   drive
    (All irregular verbs.)
13. fast   hard   early
    (All adjectives and adverbs.)
14. Thunderbird   Jaguar   Mustang
    (Cars named after animals.)
15. David   Hugh   Bob
    (All start and end with the same letter.)

Game No. 21 – Find the connection game (2)

1. Christopher Robin   Eeyore   Piglet
   (All friends of Winnie the Pooh.)
2. The Lion King   Cats   Beauty and the Beast
   (All musicals about animals.)
3. Queen's Park Victoria   Seven Sisters
   (All underground stations in London with a female connection.)
4. The Eagles   Cat Stevens   Boomtown Rats
   (All have animals in their names.)
5. scissors   parachute   high heels
   (All invented by Leonardo Di Vinci.)
6. Uranus   Neptune   Pluto
   (All planets that had metals named after them.)
7. e-mail   post   hand
   (All English words which are the same in German.)
8. dancing   gown   blitz
   (All words go with 'ballroom'.)
9. bread   forward   rock and
   (All words go with 'roll'.)
10. Barack Obama   Bill Clinton   Ronald Reagan
    (All left-handed.)
11. Ukraine   Belarus   Latvia
    (Formerly parts of the Soviet Union.)
12. Hyde   Regent's   Green
    (All names of parks in London.)
13. Lionel Richie   The Monkees   Def Leppard
    (Names containing animals.)
14. Red Hot Chilli Peppers Bread   Meatloaf
    (Food.)
15. daisies   chrysanthemums   sunflowers
    (All subjects for Vincent Van Gogh paintings.)

Game No. 23 – Who wants to be an (English) millionaire?

Question 1
   Where does the Queen live? – Buckingham Palace
Question 2
   Who lives at 10 Downing Street? – Prime Minister
Question 3
   Which river flows through London? – The Thames
Question 4
   The Beatles came from which famous English city? – Liverpool
Question 5
   Wimbledon in London is famous for what? – Tennis
Question 6
   Where are the crown jewels kept? – Tower of London

Question 7
   Who married Prince Charles? – Camilla Parker-Bowles
Question 8
   How old must someone be in Britain to vote? – 18
Question 9
   How old must someone be in Britain to buy alcohol? – 18
Question 10
   Margaret Thatcher was the leader of which political party? – The Conservative Party
Tiebreaker
   Glasgow, Manchester, Birmingham, Portsmouth

Game No. 27 – Percentages game (1)

1. 29% of men and 16% of women admit to doing this in the shower. **singing**
2. 47% of men and 32% of women have admitting to doing this in their cars in the last twelve months. **telephoning**
3. 32% of women, but only 8% of men say they do this on holiday. **send postcards**
4. 33% of men and 32% of women say they have done this in a shop in the last five years. **complained**
5. 51% of women over 50 and 32% of men over 50 say they do this on a regular basis. **lie about their age**
6. Over 50% of both men and women say they never do this in a restaurant. **complain**
7. 35% of married men, but only 5% of married women say they have done this within the last 10 years. **forgotten their partner's birthday**
8. 64% of women and 34% of men say they would never do this on a beach. **go naked**
9. 37% of women and 39% of men say they have done this in the sea. **swam naked**
10. 16% of women and 19% of men say, if they could have their time again, they wouldn't do this. **get married**

Game No. 27 – Percentages game (2)

1. Japan has **10%** of the active volcanoes in the world.
2. Close to **73%** of girls in Bangladesh are married by the age of 18.
3. Watermelons are **96%** water.
4. In the USA, **32%** of employees eat lunch and work at the same time.
5. **44%** of American adults go on a diet each year.
6. **75%** of divorced women eventually remarry.
7. **40%** of dog and cat owners carry pictures of their pets in their wallets.
8. **33%** of all food in the world intended for human consumption is lost or wasted.
9. **25%** of the world's construction cranes are currently in Dubai.
10. **90%** of an iceberg is underwater.

Game No. 28 – How long quiz

1.	How long did it take to clear Ground Zero?	**8 months, 19 days**
2.	How long is the Grand Canyon?	**446 km**
3.	How long did it take to build the Eiffel Tower?	**2 years, 2 months**
4.	How long was the first moonwalk?	**Two and half hours**
5.	What is the world record for holding your breath under water?	**22 minutes**
6.	How long is the Channel Tunnel?	**50 km**
7.	How long is a marathon to the nearest kilometre?	**42 km**
8.	How long is a round in a professional boxing match?	**Three minutes**
9.	How long is the half-time break in a football match?	**15 minutes**
10.	How long is a fortnight?	**14 days**

Game No. 29 – Multiple-choice quiz (1) – The name game

1. c. going up and down
2. a. making fun of you
3. c. to the toilet
4. a. stop it
5. b. a softie
6. c. slim Jim
7. a. it loses momentum and slowly stops
8. b. someone who can do a lot of different jobs well
9. b. doesn't believe you
10. c. a smart Alec
11. a. plain Jane
12. c. steady Eddy
13. b. a shrinking Violet
14. b. as happy as Larry

Game No. 29 – Multiple-choice (2) – Colloquial English quiz

1. a. to bed
2. b. giving up
3. b. very nervous
4. a. sick or tired
5. b. died
6. c. his colleague drank a lot
7. b. making fun of you
8. a. being sick
9. c. very easy
10. b. very mean
11. c. the police
12. a. pregnant
13. b. in prison

Game No. 29 – Multiple-choice (3) – Just a job

1. b. your shoes
2. a. clothes
3. b. sell your possessions
4. b. dead bodies
5. c. dead animals
6. c. in a police station
7. c. wood
8. b. psychological problems
9. a. sick
10. b. a worker who doesn't do the job properly
11. a. repair your clothes
12. c. pour you a drink
13. b. at the door of a nightclub
14. a. dig holes
15. c. make furniture

Game No. 29 – Multiple-choice (4) – General knowledge

1. b. London Road
2. c. Birmingham
3. b. Prince Charles
4. b. car racing
5. a. Paul & Ringo
6. b. ostrich
7. a. true
8. a. true
9. a. e
10. a. true
11. a. Polish
12. c. both the same
13. c. Everest
14. a. left
15. b. Athens

Game No. 29 – Multiple-choice (5) – Certified success

1. a. a birth certificate
2. b. a death certificate
3. a. Driver and Vehicle Licensing Agency
4. b. 'A' Levels
5. b. false
6. a. true
7. a. true
8. b. false

9. c. a sick note
10. b. Church of England
11. b. an absolute certainty
12. a. MOT certificate
13. b. trading certificate
14. a. true

Game No. 30 – German/English vocabulary quiz (1)

1. Notausgang – emergency exit
2. Mutterschaftsurlaub – maternity leave
3. Mädchenname – maiden name
4. Hochzeitstag – wedding anniversary
5. Mehrwertsteuer – value added tax
6. Kindergeld – family allowance
7. Aufenthaltserlaubnis – residence permit
8. Kaiserschnitt – caesarean section
9. Doppelgänger – double
10. Fangfrage – trick question

Game No. 30 – German/English vocabulary quiz (2)

1. Teufelskreis – vicious circle
2. Brückentag – bridge day
3. Ausbildung – apprenticeship
4. vor Ort – on site
5. Blockflöte – recorder
6. Einwegflasche – disposable bottle
7. Pfand – deposit
8. Kontoüberziehung – overdraft
9. Girokonto – current account
10. Baugenehmigung – planning permission

Game No. 30 – German/English vocabulary quiz (3)

1. Kopfsalat – lettuce
2. Kopf hoch! – chin up
3. Kopf an Kopf – neck and neck
4. Kopf runter! – duck!
5. aus dem Kopf – by heart
6. Kopf oder Zahl? – heads or tails?
7. Kopfschmerzen – headache
8. auf dem Kopf stehen – to stand on your head
9. mit dem Kopf stoßen – to nut
10. Kopfball – header

Game No. 30 – German/English vocabulary quiz (4)

1. Buggy – pushchair
2. Zylinder – tophat
3. Nichtraucher- non-smoker
4. Silvester – New Year's Eve
5. unvorhergesehen – unforeseen
6. Perücke – wig
7. Bauchnabel – belly button
8. Kreuzfahrt – cruise
9. Quittung – receipt
10. Achterbahn – rollercoaster

Game No. 30 – German/English (impossible!) vocabulary quiz (5)

1. leblos – inanimate
2. reparieren – (to) overhaul
3. Dachboden – attic
4. spotten – (to) jeer
5. staunen – (to) gape
6. verhindern – (to) thwart
7. Arbeitskittel – a smock
8. Trödelmarkt – jumble sale
9. rütteln – (to) jolt
10. Weisheitszahn – wisdom tooth

Make your own games

50/50 game

Team A		Team B	
1. _____		1. _____	
_____ / _____		_____ / _____	
2. _____		2. _____	
_____ / _____		_____ / _____	
3. _____		3. _____	
_____ / _____		_____ / _____	
4. _____		4. _____	
_____ / _____		_____ / _____	
5. _____		5. _____	
_____ / _____		_____ / _____	
6. _____		6. _____	
_____ / _____		_____ / _____	
7. _____		7. _____	
_____ / _____		_____ / _____	
8. _____		8. _____	
_____ / _____		_____ / _____	
9. _____		9. _____	
_____ / _____		_____ / _____	
10. _____		10. _____	
_____ / _____		_____ / _____	

Numbers quiz

Team Name: _____

Questions	Answers	Points
1.		
2.		
3.		
4.		
5.		
6.		
7.		
8.		
9.		
10.		
11.		
12.		
13.		
14.		
15.		
	Team Score:	

Odd man out

1.				
2.				
3.				
4.				
5.				
6.				
7.				
8.				
9.				
10.				
11.				
12.				
13.				
14.				
15.				

One minute all-out

	Letter	Category
1.		
2.		
3.		
4.		
5.		
6.		
7.		
8.		
9.		
10.		
11.		
12.		
13.		
14.		
15.		
16.		
17.		
18.		
19.		
20.		
21.		
22.		
23.		
24.		
25.		
26.		

Name the day

Event	Date
1.	
2.	
3.	
4.	
5.	
6.	
7.	
8.	
9.	
10.	

How old were they?

Name	Age	Points
1.		
2.		
3.		
4.		
5.		
6.		
7.		
8.		
9.		
10.		
	Team total:	

The choice is yours

	You	Your opponent
1.		
2.		
3.		
4.		
5.		
6.		
7.		
8.		
9.		
10.		
11.		
12.		
13.		
14.		
15.		
Your score:		